30 minute
VEGETARIAN

30 minute
VEGETARIAN

contents

30 mins

All the recipes in this book can be prepared and cooked in under 30 minutes. Some recipes may require a little additional standing or cooling time to reach perfection, but the hard work can be done in 30 minutes or less.

introduction

Poor old vegetables suffer from an unfortunate image problem. Heavily pushed as being good for us, there is an unspoken assumption that eating them is a necessary yet unpleasant chore. Generations of mothers have felt compelled to insist that there will be no ice-cream until the broccoli is eaten. Sadly, many of us don't discover a taste for vegetables until we're adults. By avoiding vegetables, we are not just depriving ourselves of the health-giving nutrients they contain, but also of the life-enhancing pleasure of eating them, and enjoying the range of amazing flavours, uses and textures that they offer.

There is no cuisine that does not rest on a foundation of vegetables. While many of us think of protein as the main event and vegetables as something to go on the side, this is a recent development, allowed only by intensive farming and supermarket convenience. For most of history, meat and fish were an unpredictable luxury, and vegetables, fruit and grains — those things that we could grow for ourselves — were the staples that kept us alive.

Before the refrigerator, diet was inevitably dictated by the seasons, the harvest, climate and location; we ate what we could grow and made the most of what we had. Now, air-freight and cold storage provide a level of convenience and choice that would have been unimaginable to the home cook of an earlier age. Dining on strawberries mid-winter or peas all year round would have been the preserve of the immensely wealthy, or simply impossible. We may have gained a luxury, but we have lost something much richer — a connection to our food and a real sense of place. Travel around much of Asia or southern Europe and what you will still find is a cuisine that isn't so much national as regional. While the basics may be similar, the detail of each dish will reflect the particular ingredients at hand as the dish was created. From valley to valley, the micro-climate changes; the clever gardener plants what will thrive, so the basket of fresh vegetables collected for each meal is unique to its place.

Many people have recognised an imbalance in their way of eating and are modifying the amount of meat dishes included in their diets. The discovery of vegetarian food often begins in this way. As people gain confidence, experiment more and discover the pleasures of cooking vegetarian foods they often welcome increased vitality and say goodbye to weight problems.

The recipes in this book are for anyone who loves preparing, serving and eating good food. It is neither a diet nor a health-food book, but is designed to expand the menu possibilities, to show that one can be a connoisseur of good food, a fine cook and a vegetarian.

spring

Spring is a time of new beginnings. There's a vital urgency in the air, a smell of nature bursting back to life in all its soft, green glory. The freshness of spring reawakens the physical and sensual, reconnecting us to senses that have lain dormant throughout the winter months. Instead of long, slow meals that fill us up and keep us warm, we want snap, crackle and pop. Rather than vegetables simmered to a yielding softness, we want to feel that bite of spring on our palate as well as in the air. The move away from the sustaining root vegetables to tender, sweet baby greens is as natural as the growing seasons themselves.

At the first sign of spring, market gardens and fields explode into new, green life. Pea vines are laden with fat, juicy pods full of sweet, green peas. Beans of every variety, but especially broad beans, are at their tender, lively best. The first crop of tender asparagus is pushing its way through the soil to the light. Fresh herbs are back on the menu, thriving wherever they are planted.

Plenty is not the only gift of spring; it also heralds the return of variety and quality. Both markets and supermarkets offer an almost bewildering array of tempting goodies to choose from. You may find yourself lugging home such a pile of fresh produce that it's difficult to cook and eat it all before it is past its best. The essence of spring is the freshness of its offerings, the brand-spanking newness of it all. Capture this by shopping selectively and often; look for a local market, make use of your local grocer, let the experts do the sourcing for you. Buying little and often reconnects us to an earlier time when we stocked our table with the fruits of our own labour. Meals were made with what could be picked fresh from the garden, and profligacy was a luxury afforded to the few.

Beyond the benefits of crispness and flavour, truly fresh food offers a range of vitamins and minerals that no tablet could ever hope to imitate. There's no quicker way to health than stocking your house with the best seasonal food. And by supporting your local greengrocer, you get the added bonus of keeping your local community alive with choice and variety.

Simplicity is the only rule in making the most of spring vegetables. Clean, crisp flavours are best achieved by taking a light approach with both method and seasoning. Rather than treating the vegetables as a background for other foods, look for simple ways to enhance their natural sweetness and crisp vitality. Purity of flavour and a delicious variety of fresh, baby produce are the great gifts of generous, bountiful spring.

23 mins

Green stir-fry with sesame and soy

SERVES 4 ✳ **PREPARATION TIME: 15 MINUTES** ✳ **COOKING TIME: 8 MINUTES**

Many Asian greens are interchangeable as far as taste goes, and it is their appearance and freshness that determine the ones to use. Pak choy (bok choy) is readily available, but other Asian greens also work well.

2 tablespoons light soy sauce
1 tablespoon hoisin sauce
1 tablespoon vegetable stock
2 tablespoons vegetable oil
1 teaspoon sesame oil
4 garlic cloves, finely sliced
2 teaspoons julienned ginger
2 kg (4 bunches) baby pak choy (bok choy), cut into quarters, well washed and drained
200 g (7 oz) mangetout (snow peas), trimmed
200 g (7 oz) sugar snap peas, trimmed
2 tablespoons bamboo shoots, julienned
jasmine rice, to serve

1. In a small jug mix together the light soy sauce, hoisin sauce and stock.

2. Heat a wok over a high heat and add the vegetables and sesame oil. Stir-fry the garlic, ginger and pak choy for 3 minutes. Add the mangetout, sugar snap peas and bamboo shoots and stir-fry for a further 5 minutes. Pour in the sauce, and gently toss until the sauce has reduced slightly to coat the just tender vegetables. Serve immediately with jasmine rice.

Pea and asparagus saffron risotto

SERVES 4 ✳ **PREPARATION TIME: 7 MINUTES** ✳ **COOKING TIME: 23 MINUTES**

Asparagus cooks beautifully on the chargrill. Its flavour is intensified and it tends to stay crisp and bright. Many believe that the biggest benefit is in the timing — where a matter of seconds can be critical when steaming or boiling, grilling offers a lot more leeway.

Remove the woody end of the asparagus.

Cook the spears for 1–2 minutes in simmering water.

pinch saffron threads
2 tablespoons olive oil
1 onion, finely chopped
440 g (15½ oz/2 cups) risotto rice
1.5 litres (52 fl oz/6 cups) hot vegetable stock
450 g (1 lb) fresh peas (in the pod), or 235 g (8½ oz/1½ cups) frozen peas, blanched
175 g (6 oz/1 bunch) asparagus, cut into bite sized pieces and blanched
30 g (1 oz) parmesan cheese, finely grated

1. Put 3 tablespoons of boiling water into a small bowl, and add the saffron threads. Set aside until required.

2. Heat the oil in a large, heavy-based saucepan. Add the onion and cook over medium heat for 3-4 minutes, or until soft and transparent. Add the rice stirring until well coated in oil.

3. Add about 4 tablespoons (2 fl oz/⅓ cup) of the hot stock to the rice, stirring constantly. When it has absorbed into the rice, add another 4 tablespoons of the hot stock. Keep adding stock, stirring between each addition, until the rice is tender and creamy. This will take about 20 minutes. Add the saffron and the liquid about halfway through adding the stock.

4. About 5 minutes before the rice is ready, add the peas and asparagus to the rice so that they will cook with the last addition of stock. Remove from the heat, and stir in the parmesan. Serve immediately, and top with freshly ground black pepper.

23 mins

Broad bean, feta and preserved lemon salad

SERVES 4 ∗ **PREPARATION TIME: 15 MINUTES** ∗ **COOKING TIME: 8 MINUTES**

Preserved lemons are a key ingredient in North African cooking and add a delicious sweet-sour flavour when added to dishes. It is important to rinse the lemon quarters and remove the pulp, otherwise they will remain overpoweringly salty.

350 g (12 oz/2¼ cups) frozen broad (fava) beans
1 red pepper (capsicum), finely sliced
100 g (3½ oz/ ⅔ cup) firm feta cheese, cut into cubes
1 tablespoon za'atar (thyme, sesame seed and sumac spice blend)
¼ small red onion, finely sliced
125 g (4½ oz) yellow baby tomatoes, cut in half
¼ preserved lemon, pulp removed, washed and finely sliced
100 g (3½ oz) mixed salad leaves

Orange dressing
2 teaspoons grated orange zest
2 tablespoons orange juice
2 tablespoons olive oil
1 teaspoon honey
1 teaspoon za'atar (thyme, sesame seed and sumac spice blend)

1. Bring a saucepan of water to the boil. Add the broad beans and bring back to the boil. Cook for 5 minutes, drain, refresh under cold running water and peel the outer skins from the beans.

2. Meanwhile, in another small saucepan, blanch the red pepper in boiling water for 1 minute, then drain, refresh and drain again. Sprinkle the feta cubes with the za'atar to coat on all sides. Combine all the dressing ingredients.

3. Put the broad beans, pepper, onion and tomatoes in a large bowl. Add the preserved lemon. Pour over the dressing and toss. Add the feta cubes and toss gently. Put the salad leaves on serving plates and pile the combined mixture on top.

preserved lemons

A Middle Eastern ingredient made by steeping lemons in salt and lemon juice, and leaving them to mature for at least a month before use. Preserved lemons can last over a year without being refrigerated.

30 mins

Egg noodles with Asian greens and glazed tofu

SERVES 4 * **PREPARATION TIME: 15 MINUTES + MARINATING TIME**
COOKING TIME: 15 MINUTES

Egg noodles are thick Chinese noodles that are very filling and perfect for stir-fries. They are found in both the chilled section and on the shelves of the supermarket.

300 g (10½ oz) firm tofu
60 ml (¼ cup) kecap manis (sweet soy sauce)
1 tablespoon mushroom soy sauce
1 tablespoon vegetarian oyster sauce
1 teaspoon sesame oil
1 tablespoon peanut oil
2 garlic cloves, crushed
1 tablespoon grated fresh ginger
1 onion, cut into wedges
450 g (1 bunch) flowering pak choy (choy sum), roughly chopped
500 g (1 bunch) baby pak choi (bok choy), roughly chopped
450 g (1 lb) fresh egg (hokkien) noodles, separated
2 tablespoons peanut oil, extra

1. Cut the tofu into 1cm (½ inch) thick slices and place in a shallow, non-metallic dish. Mix together the kecap manis, soy and oyster sauces and pour over the tofu. Leave to marinate for about 15 minutes, then drain and reserve the marinade.

2. Heat the oils in a wok over medium heat, add the garlic, ginger and onion and stir-fry until the onion is soft. Remove. Add the green vegetables to the wok and stir-fry until just wilted. Remove. Add the separated noodles and the reserved marinade and stir-fry until heated through. Remove from the wok and divide among four plates.

3. Fry the tofu in the extra oil until it is browned on both sides. Serve the noodles topped with the tofu, green vegetables and onion mixture.

tofu
Tofu itself is very bland, but lends itself well to marinating and cooking with flavours such as garlic, ginger, soy sauce and chilli.

Three ways with peas

Fresh peas are little gems of sweet goodness. Peas also freeze very well, which means that they are available all year round, and their gentle flavour makes them extremely versatile.

Pea and potato samosas

MAKES: 10 ＊ **PREPARATION TIME: 20 MINUTES** ＊ **COOKING TIME: 10 MINUTES**

Blend 30 g (1 oz) ghee with 200 g (7 oz/1¾ cups) plain (all-purpose) flour in a food processor until combined. Add a large pinch of salt and 100ml (3½ fl oz) warm water and process until the dough forms a ball. Knead 4-5 times, then cover and chill until required. Shell 200 g (7 oz) peas to give 70 g (2½ oz/½ cup). Cook the peas in boiling water, then drain. Heat 20 g (¾ oz) ghee in a frying pan over medium heat. Fry ½ finely chopped small onion, 85 g (3 oz/½ cup) diced potato, 2 crushed garlic cloves, 2 teaspoons each of grated fresh ginger and garam masala, ½ teaspoon each of ground cumin and ground coriander, and ¼ teaspoon each of turmeric and chilli powder for 5-6 minutes, stirring often. Stir in the peas. Roll out the dough to 1 mm (¹⁄₁₆ inch) thick and cut out ten 10 cm (4 inch) rounds. Put some of the pea mixture in the centre of each round and brush the edges with water. Fold over the pastry and press the edges well to seal. Fill a deep-fryer, wok or heavy-based saucepan one-third full of vegetable oil and heat to 180°C (350°F) or until a cube of bread dropped into the oil browns in 15 seconds. Deep-fry the samosas in the oil until browned, about 2 minutes. Serve with 250 g (9 oz/1 cup) plain yoghurt mixed with 2 teaspoons chopped mint and ¼ teaspoon each of ground coriander and ground cumin.

Mushy peas with fennel and spring onions

SERVES: 4 ＊ **PREPARATION TIME: 10 MINUTES** ＊ **COOKING TIME: 20 MINUTES**

Shell 850 g (1 lb 14 oz) peas to give 320 g (11¼ oz/2 cups). Peel 1 small potato and cut into 2 cm (¾ inch) cubes. Heat 20 g (¾ oz) butter and 1 tablespoon oil in a large saucepan over medium-low heat and fry 1 thinly sliced baby fennel bulb for 3-4 minutes, or until soft. Add the peas, potato, 250 ml (9 fl oz/1 cup) milk and enough water to just cover the vegetables. Simmer for about 15 minutes, until the peas and potato are tender and the liquid has evaporated. Stir regularly towards the end of the cooking time to prevent sticking. Season with salt, pepper and a good pinch of ground nutmeg. Add 4 thinly sliced spring onions (scallions) and 1 small handful chopped fennel leaves. Roughly break up the mixture using a potato masher or fork. Serve hot, drizzled with extra virgin olive oil.

Risi e bisi (rice and peas)

SERVES: 4 ＊ **PREPARATION TIME: 15 MINUTES** ＊ **COOKING TIME: 15 MINUTES**

Shell 800 g (1 lb 12 oz) peas to give 300 g (10½ oz/2 cups). Heat 1 litre (35 fl oz/4 cups) vegetable stock in a saucepan. Meanwhile heat 55 g (2 oz) butter in a large, deep frying pan over low heat. Fry 6 sliced spring onions (scallions). Add 325 g (11½ oz/1½ cups) arborio rice and stir to coat. Add a ladleful of hot stock and simmer until it is almost absorbed. Add the peas and another ladleful of stock and cook until the stock is almost absorbed. Continue in this way until the rice is tender but al dente. This will take 15-20 minutes. There should still be enough liquid in the pan for it to flow. Stir through 30 g (1 oz) butter, 50 g (1¾ oz/½ cup) shredded parmesan cheese and 2 tablespoons of chopped fresh mint. Season with salt and freshly ground black pepper and set aside for 1 minute before serving

Mangetout salad with Japanese dressing

SERVES 4-6 ✳ **PREPARATION TIME: 15 MINUTES** ✳ **COOKING TIME: 1 MINUTE**

mangetout (snow peas) are one of the true treats of the spring harvest. Left to linger in the fridge, they will quickly wilt, so for best results, buy them on the day you plan to use them. Top and tail them before cooking.

250 g (9 oz) mangetout (snowpeas), trimmed
iced water
50 g (1¾ oz) mangetout (snowpeas) sprouts
1 small red pepper (capsicum), cut into matchsticks
½ teaspoon dashi granules (dried seaweed and fish flakes granules)
1 tablespoon soy sauce
1 tablespoon mirin (sweet Japanese rice wine)
1 teaspoon soft brown sugar
1 garlic clove, crushed
1 teaspoon very finely chopped ginger
¼ teaspoon sesame oil
1 tablespoon vegetable oil
1 tablespoon toasted sesame seeds

1. Bring a saucepan of water to the boil, add the mangetout and cook for 1 minute. Drain, then plunge into a bowl of iced water for 2 minutes. Drain well and combine with the sprouts and pepper in a serving bowl.

2. Dissolve the dashi granules in 1½ tablespoons (¾ fl oz) of hot water and whisk in a small bowl with the soy sauce, mirin, sugar, garlic, ginger, sesame oil, vegetable oil and half of the toasted sesame seeds. Pour over the mangetout mixture and toss well. Season to taste, and serve sprinkled with the remaining sesame seeds.

mangetout

There are two types of mangetout: those with a flat thin pod (snow peas), and those with a more rounded pod (sugar snap or snap peas). Both types are best when perfectly fresh; they are not really designed to be stored at all. Left to linger in the fridge, they will quickly wilt, so for best results, buy them on the day you plan to use them. Top and tail them before cooking.

Broad bean rotollo with salad greens

SERVES: 4 ＊ **PREPARATION TIME: 15 MINUTES** ＊ **COOKING TIME: 15 MINUTES**

Rotollo
750 g (1 lb 10 oz), broad (fava) beans shelled to give 275 g (9¾ oz/1½ cups)
4 eggs
4 egg yolks
2 teaspoons finely chopped mint
2 teaspoons finely chopped basil
20 g (¾ oz) butter
80 g (2¾ oz) grated pecorino cheese

Salad
1½ tablespoons pine nuts
1 tablespoon chopped basil
80 ml (2½ fl oz/⅓ cup) olive oil
2 tablespoons lemon juice
2 baby cos (romaine) lettuces, trimmed
2 chicory (witlof/Belgian endive), trimmed, preferably purple

1. To make the rotollo, bring a medium saucepan of water to the boil. Add a large pinch of salt and the broad beans and simmer for 2 minutes. Drain and plunge into iced water. Drain and peel the skins off the beans, discarding the skins.

2. Preheat the oven to 160°C (315°F/ Gas 2-3). Beat the eggs, egg yolks, mint and basil together and season with salt and freshly ground black pepper. Melt half the butter in a 20 cm (8 inch) non-stick frying or crepe pan over medium-high heat. Pour in half the egg mixture and cook until the base has set but the top is still a little runny.

3. Slide the omelette from the pan onto a sheet of baking paper. Scatter half the pecorino and half the broad beans over the surface. Using the baking paper as a guide, gently roll the omelette into a tight sausage. Roll the baking paper around the omelette and tie both ends with string to prevent it from unrolling. Place on a baking sheet. Make another roll with the remaining ingredients and put on the baking sheet. Bake for 8 minutes. Remove from the oven, set aside for 2-3 minutes, then unwrap and set aside to cool.

4. Meanwhile put the pine nuts in a small dry saucepan over medium heat and toast, stirring and tossing constantly, for 4-5 minutes, or until the nuts are golden-brown and fragrant. Tip the nuts into a bowl so they do not cook further from the residual heat, and allow to cool.

5. To make the salad, put 1 tablespoon of the pine nuts, the basil, olive oil and lemon juice in a small food processor or blender and process until smooth. Season with salt and freshly ground black pepper. Put the cos and chicory leaves in a bowl and dress with 2 tablespoons of the dressing.

6. Slice the rotollo into rounds and scatter over the salad, along with the remaining pine nuts. Drizzle the remaining dressing over the top and serve.

Roll up the filled omelette, using the baking paper to help you.

Roll the baking paper around the omelette and tie with string.

30 mins

Stuffed artichokes

SERVES 4 ✳ **PREPARATION TIME: 5 MINUTES** ✳ **COOKING TIME: 25 MINUTES**

The globe artichoke is a member of the thistle family and the parts that we eat are the immature flower head, the heart and the tender stem immediately below. Artichokes oxidize when their cut surfaces are exposed to air or aluminium. This causes browning and a metallic taste, but these effects can be minimized, by placing artichoke pieces in acidulated water.

40 g (1½ oz/¼ cup) roasted
    almonds
4 young globe artichokes
150 g (5½ oz) fresh ricotta cheese
2 garlic cloves, crushed
80 g (2¾ oz/1 cup) fresh course
    breadcrumbs
1 teaspoon finely grated lemon zest
50 g (1¾ oz/½ cup) grated
    parmesan cheese
1 small handful chopped flat-leaf
    (Italian) parsley
1 tablespoon olive oil
2 tablespoons butter
2 tablespoons lemon juice

1. Remove any tough outer leaves from the artichokes. Cut across the artichokes, about 3cm (1¼ inches) from the top, and trim the stalks, leaving about 2cm (¾ inch). Rub with lemon and put in a bowl of cold water with a little lemon juice to prevent the artichokes from turning brown.

2. Combine the almonds, ricotta, garlic, breadcrumbs, lemon zest, parmesan and parsley in a bowl and season. Gently separate the artichoke leaves and push the filling in between them. Place the artichokes carefully in a steamer and drizzle with the olive oil. Steam for 20 minutes, or until tender (test with a metal skewer). Remove and cook under a hot grill (broiler) for about 5 minutes to brown the filling.

3. Melt the butter in a saucepan, remove from the heat and stir in the lemon juice. Arrange the artichokes on a serving plate, drizzle with the butter sauce and season well.

Hold the artichoke head in one hand, snap off the stem and remove any tough fibres. Remove any tough outer leaves, then simmer in boiling water.

25 mins

Pasta primavera

SERVES 4 ＊ **PREPARATION TIME: 15 MINUTES** ＊ **COOKING TIME: 10 MINUTES**

In Italy, pasta primavera heralds the arrival of springtime. This variation combines broad beans, asparagus, green beans, and peas — the best of green spring vegetables — in a light, creamy sauce. Fennel adds a delicious twist.

120 g (4 oz) broad (fava) beans,
   fresh or frozen
150 g (5½ oz) asparagus, cut into
   short lengths
350 g (12 oz) fresh tagliatelle
100 g (3½ oz) green beans, cut into
   short lengths
120 g (4 ¼ oz/¾ cup) peas, fresh or
   frozen
30 g (1 oz) salted butter
1 small fennel bulb, thinly sliced
375 ml (13 fl oz/1½ cups) thick
   (double/heavy) cream
2 tablespoons grated parmesan
   cheese, plus extra, to serve

1. Bring a large saucepan of water to the boil. Add 1 teaspoon of salt, the broad beans and asparagus and simmer for 3 minutes.

2. Remove the vegetables with a slotted spoon and set them aside. Add the tagliatelle to the saucepan and, when it has softened, stir in the beans and the peas (if you're using frozen peas, add them a few minutes later). Cook for about 4 minutes, or until the pasta is *al dente*.

3. Meanwhile, heat the butter in a large frying pan. Add the fennel and cook over moderately low heat without colouring for 5 minutes. Add the cream, season with salt and pepper and cook at a low simmer.

4. Peel the skins from the broad beans. Drain the pasta, green beans and peas and add them to the frying pan. Add 2 tablespoons of parmesan and the broad beans and asparagus. Toss lightly to coat. Serve immediately with extra parmesan.

Three ways with asparagus

For the true food lover, the coming of spring is heralded by the first, slender stalks of asparagus. Some prefer asparagus al dente, but the softness of well-cooked stems pairs divinely with goat's cheese in a tasty salad. Hollandaise sauce is the classic accompaniment for steamed asparagus and egg and asparagus always goes well with lemon, as in this delicious light soup.

Asparagus orange salad

SERVES: 4 * **PREPARATION TIME: 15 MINUTES** * **COOKING TIME: 2 MINUTES**

Cook 300 g (10½ oz) thin asparagus spears in boiling water for 1-2 minutes, or until just tender. Rinse under cold water to cool, then combine with 50 g (1¾ oz/1½ cups) watercress, ½ small red onion, very thinly sliced and a segmented orange on a serving dish. Combine 1 tablespoon orange juice, 1 teaspoon finely grated orange zest, 1 teaspoon sugar, 1 tablespoon red wine vinegar and 2 teaspoons poppy seeds in a jug. Whisk in 2 tablespoons olive oil with a fork until combined and drizzle over the salad. Crumble 60 g (2¼ oz) soft goat's cheese over the salad and season to taste with salt and pepper.

Asparagus and hollandaise sauce

SERVES: 4 * **PREPARATION TIME: 10 MINUTES** * **COOKING TIME: 10 MINUTES**

Whisk together 1 egg yolk and 1 teaspoon each of water, lemon juice and white wine vinegar and put in the top of a double boiler over simmering water, making sure it does not touch the water. Whisk for 1 minute, or until thick and foaming. Slowly pour in 60 ml (2 fl oz/¼ cup) melted unsalted butter, whisking constantly. Continue whisking for about 1 minute, until thick and creamy, then season with salt and pepper. Put 20 trimmed asparagus spears in a steamer basket over simmering water. Cover and steam until al dente (4-8 minutes, depending on the size and age of the asparagus). Group the asparagus into 4 bundles. Serve with the hollandaise sauce spooned over the bundles.

Asparagus soup

SERVES: 4 * **PREPARATION TIME: 10 MINUTES** * **COOKING TIME: 15 MINUTES**

Trim and discard the woody ends from 750 g (1 lb 10 oz) fresh asparagus spears and cut into 2 cm (¾ inch) lengths. Place in a large saucepan and add 500 ml (17 fl oz/2 cups) of vegetable stock. Cover and bring to the boil, then cook for 10 minutes, or until the asparagus is tender. Transfer the asparagus and the hot stock to a blender or food processor and puree in batches until smooth. Melt 30 g (1 oz) butter in the saucepan over low heat, add 1 tablespoon plain (all-purpose) flour flour, then cook, stirring, for about 1 minute, or until pale and foaming. Remove from the heat and gradually add another 500ml (2 cups) of vegetable stock, stirring until smooth after each addition. When all the stock has been added, return the saucepan to the heat, bring to the boil, then simmer for 2 minutes. Add the asparagus puree to the pan and stir until combined. When heated through, stir in ½ teaspoon finely grated lemon zest and season with salt and cracked black pepper. Garnish with extra lemon zest.

30 mins

Pea, egg and ricotta curry

SERVES: 4 ✳ **PREPARATION TIME: 10 MINUTES** ✳ **COOKING TIME: 20 MINUTES**

This is an adaptation of the classic Egg Curry (or Anda Curry) from Northern India. If baked ricotta is unavailable try using paneer instead, which is an Indian cottage cheese available from good supermarkets.

4 hard-boiled eggs
½ teaspoon ground turmeric
2 small onions
25 g (4½ oz) baked ricotta cheese
45 ml (1½ fl oz) ghee or oil
1 bay leaf
1 teaspoon finely chopped garlic
1½ teaspoons ground coriander
1½ teaspoons garam masala
½ teaspoon chilli powder (optional)
125 g (4½ oz/½ cup) tinned peeled, chopped tomatoes
1 tablespoon tomato purée (paste)
1 tablespoon plain yoghurt
80 g (2¾ oz/½ cup) frozen peas
2 tablespoons finely chopped coriander (cilantro) leaves

1. Peel the eggs and coat them with the turmeric. Finely chop the onion and cut the ricotta into 1 cm (½ inch) cubes.

2. Melt the ghee in a large saucepan and cook the eggs over medium heat for 2 minutes until they are light brown, stirring constantly. Set aside.

3. Add the bay leaf, onion and garlic to the pan and cook over medium-high heat for 5 minutes, or until the mixture is soft and pale gold. Add the coriander, garam masala and chilli powder, if using, and cook for 1-2 minutes until fragrant.

4. Add the tomatoes, tomato purée and 125 ml (4 fl oz/½ cup) water. Cover and simmer for 5 minutes. Return the eggs to the pan with the ricotta, yoghurt, peas and ¼ teaspoon salt and cook for 5 minutes. Remove the bay leaf, sprinkle with the coriander and serve immediately.

Mango fool

SERVES: 4 ✳ **PREPARATION TIME: 15 MINUTES** ✳ **COOKING TIME: NIL**

When you have a lovely, ripe mango to hand it's hard not to just eat it right there and then and forget making a dessert. But mango marries wonderfully with yoghurt and cream, making a perfect fool, which is both light and tasty.

2 very ripe mangoes
250 ml (9 fl oz/1 cup) Greek-style
   yoghurt
80 ml (2 ½ fl oz/⅓ cup) cream

1. Take the flesh off the mangoes. The easiest way to do this is to slice down either side of the stone so you have two 'cheeks'. Make crisscross cuts through the mango flesh on each cheek, almost through to the skin, then turn each cheek inside out and slice the flesh from the skin into a bowl. Cut the rest of the flesh from the stone.

2. Purée the flesh either by using a food processor or blender, or if you don't have any of these, just mash the flesh thoroughly.

3. Put a spoonful of mango purée in the bottom of four small glasses, bowls or cups, put a spoonful of yoghurt on top and then repeat. Spoon half the cream over each serving when you have used up all the mango and yoghurt. Swirl the layers together just before you eat them.

mango

You can determine if a mango is ripe, not by its colour, which can vary, but by both its smell and feel—a ripe mango has a wonderful aroma and will yield when gently pressed. Store unripe mangoes at room temperature, then put them in the fridge when ripened.

Ginger and grapefruit puddings with mascarpone cream

SERVES: 6 ∗ PREPARATION TIME: 10 MINUTES ∗ COOKING TIME: 20 MINUTES

These puddings are ideal for spring, when anything too heavy or rich doesn't feel right. They have a light, clean flavour due to the ginger and ruby grapefruit, which is matched by a fluffy, warm sponge. Of course, if that sounds too healthy, you can add a good dollop of mascarpone cream.

1 large ruby grapefruit
40 g (1½ oz/⅓ cup) stem ginger in syrup drained, plus 3 teaspoons syrup
1½ tablespoons golden syrup or dark corn syrup
125 g (4½ oz) unsalted butter, softened
115 g (4 oz/½ cup) caster (superfine) sugar
2 eggs, at room temperature
185 g (6½ oz/1½ cups) self-raising flour
1 teaspoon ground ginger
80 ml (2½fl oz/⅓ cup) milk

Mascarpone cream
125 g (4½oz/heaped ½ cup) mascarpone cheese
125 ml (4fl oz/½ cup) cream (whipping)
1 tablespoon icing (confectioners') sugar, sifted

1. Preheat the oven to 190°C (375°F/ Gas 5). Grease 6 x 170 ml (5½ fl oz/⅔ cup) pudding moulds or ramekins.

2. Finely grate 2 teaspoons of zest from the ruby grapefruit and set aside. Slice the grapefruit around its circumference, one-third of the way down. Peel the larger piece of grapefruit, removing any white pith, and cut the flesh into six 1 cm (½ inch) slices. Squeeze 3 teaspoons of

juice from the remaining grapefruit. Finely chop the stem ginger.

3. Combine the grapefruit juice, ginger syrup and golden or corn syrup in a small bowl. Divide the mixture among the pudding moulds and top with a slice of grapefruit, trimming to fit.

4. Put the butter and sugar in a bowl and beat with electric beaters until pale and smooth. Beat in the eggs, one at a time. Sift in the flour and ground ginger, add the grapefruit zest, chopped ginger and milk and mix well. Divide the mixture among the moulds.

5. Cover each mould with foil and put them in a deep roasting tin. Pour in enough boiling water to come halfway up the side of the moulds. Cover the roasting tin with foil, sealing the edges well. Bake the puddings for 20 minutes, or until set.

6. Meanwhile to make the mascarpone cream, mix the mascarpone, cream and icing sugar in a small bowl until smooth.

7. To serve, gently invert the puddings onto serving plates and serve with the mascarpone cream.

Use scissors to trim the grapefruit to fit the moulds.

The grapefruit syrup gives the puddings a lovely moist top.

20 mins

Banana fritters in coconut batter

SERVES 6 ✳ **PREPARATION TIME: 10 MINUTES** ✳ **COOKING TIME: 10 MINUTES**

It's easy to see why this fabulous dessert is a childhood favourite — melting banana in a crispy, hot casing with hints of coconut. The warm banana smells wonderful too, adding to the pleasure, especially when served with ice cream.

100 g (3½ oz/ ½ cup) glutinous
   rice flour
100 g freshly grated coconut or
   60 g/ ⅔ cup desiccated coconut
50 g (1 ¾ oz/¼ cup) sugar
1 tablespoon sesame seeds
60 ml (¼ cup) coconut milk
6 bananas
oil, for deep-frying
ice cream, to serve

1. Place the flour, coconut, sugar, sesame seeds, coconut milk and 60ml (2 fl oz/¼ cup) water in a bowl and whisk to a smooth batter – add more water if the batter is too thick.

2. Peel the bananas and cut in half lengthways (cut each portion in half crossways if the bananas are large).

3. Fill a wok or deep heavy-based saucepan one-third full of oil and heat to 180°C (350°F), or until a cube of bread browns in 15 seconds. Dip each piece of banana into the batter, then drop gently into the hot oil. Cook in batches for 4-6 minutes, or until golden brown all over. Remove with a slotted spoon and drain on paper towels. Serve hot with ice cream.

bananas

Do not store bananas in the fridge as the skin will turn black (though this doesn't affect the taste). Bananas produce ethylene, which cause other fruit or vegetables sitting near them to ripen prematurely.

summer

Summer bursts into life in a riot of colour and turns the everyday experience of eating into a passionate treat for the senses. The sun intensifies the impact of colour and aroma, heightening sensations yet curbing appetite. The best summer food is swift and simple; effortless meals of wonderful fresh ingredients can be tossed together in no time and spread along the table for all to share. There is no better time of year to nourish yourself, in both body and soul, with crisp, light, vibrant vegetables.

Long sultry days are the essence of summer and the perfect backdrop for entertaining at home. This is the time of year when the party season really swings into gear. We're all caterers come the summer months and this is the easiest time of year to create a spectacular array of fresh delicacies. The warm weather has worked its magic in the fields and the summer harvest is a cornucopia of fresh delights.

Salad is the quintessential summer dish and salad vegetables flourish during the warmer months. Tomatoes are at their reddest and ripest; ears of corn hang heavy on the stalk; pepper, cucumber and lettuce are crisp and fresh. Eating seasonally through the summer months is easy and appealing. The beauty of summer vegetables lies in the intensity of their colour and flavour — it's as though basking in the hot sunshine has imbued them with a special sweetness.

All of this makes them perfect for creating meals that work with the weather. Long, warm days can leave you feeling languid and the idea of a big, hot meal is just too daunting. The key to creating a meal that is light and yet still satisfying is to go small on quantity but big on flavour. The perfect summer dish is one that fills you up without weighing you down.

As with all cooking, the key to getting the most out of summer vegetables lies in technique. Quick and easy are the catchwords for summer eating. When the mercury is rising, there is little appeal in stoking up the oven in an already hot house. So try a little flash-frying or just revel in the natural sweetness in a pile of fresh vegetables. Summer is finally here and it's time to celebrate this season of plenty.

Courgette flowers stuffed with Moroccan spiced chickpeas

SERVES: 4 ∗ PREPARATION TIME: 15 MINUTES ∗ COOKING TIME: 15 MINUTES

Courgette (zucchini) flowers, which are edible, do not last long once picked and are a fleeting delight of summer. They are usually stuffed, then baked or fried. Before using, remove and discard the stamen from inside the flower, wash the flower and make sure it does not harbour any insects.

150 g (5½ oz) butternut squash (pumpkin), chopped
300 g (10½ oz) tin chickpeas, drained and rinsed
2 tablespoons currants
4 red Asian shallots, finely chopped
½ teaspoon ground cumin
½ teaspoon ground cinnamon
1½ tablespoons lemon juice
2 teaspoons chopped coriander (cilantro) leaves
2 teaspoons chopped parsely
12 large courgette (zucchini) flowers with stems attached

Garlic and lemon butter
100 g (3½ oz) ghee (see tip)
4 garlic cloves, crushed
1 teaspoon ground coriander
pinch of cayenne pepper
1 tablespoon lemon juice

1. Place the squash pieces in a steamer and cover with a lid. Sit the steamer over a saucepan or wok of boiling water and steam for 5-8 minutes, or until the squash is soft. Transfer the squash to a bowl, allow to cool then mash well with a fork.

2. Meanwhile, coarsely mash the chickpeas in a separate bowl. Add the currants, shallots, cumin, cinnamon, lemon juice, coriander and parsley and season with salt and freshly ground black pepper. Fold the mashed squash through the mixture until well combined.

3. Carefully remove the stamens from inside the courgette flowers and trim the ends. Fill each flower until almost full, then gently twist the flower tips to secure the filling. Lay the stuffed flowers in the steamer so they all fit snugly in a single layer.

4. Sit the steamer over a saucepan or wok of boiling water and steam for 5-8 minutes, or until the courgette stems are just tender when tested.

5. Meanwhile, to make the garlic and lemon butter, melt the ghee in a small saucepan over medium heat. Add the garlic and ½ teaspoon of salt and sauté for 2 minutes, or until the garlic starts to turn golden brown and the butter is frothing. Add the coriander and cayenne pepper and cook 30 seconds. Stir in the lemon juice.

6. Put three stuffed courgette flowers on each plate and drizzle with some of the hot garlic and lemon butter.

Note: Ghee is clarified butter, or pure butter fat. It can be heated to higher temperatures than regular butter without burning. It is available in small tins or bars in most supermarkets.

Spoon the squash mixture, then gently twist the flower tips to secure the filling.

Saute until the garlic is golden brown and the butter is frothing.

Tunisian aubergine salad with preserved lemon

SERVES: 4 * **PREPARATION TIME: 15 MINUTES + RESTING TIME**
COOKING TIME: 15 MINUTES

Aubergine (eggplant) is common in Tunisian salads and stews. The cubed flesh may be salted for up to 24 hours to extract all the moisture, so that very little oil is required for frying. This salad is best made in advance and left for several hours for the flavours to merge.

2 large aubergines (eggplants)
125 ml (4 fl oz/½ cup) olive oil
1 teaspoon cumin seeds
2 cloves, very thinly sliced garlic
1 tablespoon currants
1 tablespoon slivered almonds
6 small plum (roma) tomatoes, quartered lengthways
1 teaspoon dried oregano
4 red bird's eye chillies, halved lengthways and seeded
2 tablespoons lemon juice
4 tablespoons chopped parsley
½ preserved or salted lemon
extra virgin olive oil to serve

1. Cut the aubergines into 2 cm (¾ inch) cubes, put in a large colander and sprinkle with 1-2 teaspoons salt. Set aside to drain in the sink for 2-3 hours. Dry with paper towels.

2. Heat half the olive oil in a large flameproof casserole dish over medium-high heat. Fry the aubergine in batches for 5-6 minutes, or until golden, adding more oil as required. Drain on crumpled paper towels.

3. Reduce the heat and add any remaining oil to the casserole dish, along with the cumin, garlic, currants and almonds. Fry for 20-30 seconds, or until the garlic starts to colour. Add the tomato and oregano and cook for 1 minute. Remove from the heat.

4. Trim the rind from the piece of preserved lemon and cut the rind into thin strips. Discard the flesh.

5. Return the aubergine to the casserole and add the chilli, lemon juice, parsley and preserved lemon rind. Toss gently and season with freshly ground black pepper. Set aside at room temperature for at least 1 hour before serving. Check the seasoning, then drizzle with extra virgin olive oil.

Add the tomato and oregano to the pan and fry for 1 minute.

Slice the rind of the preserved lemon into thin strips.

30 mins

Baked baby pattypan squash

SERVES: 4 ✳ **PREPARATION TIME: 5 MINUTES** ✳ **COOKING TIME: 25 MINUTES**

No other cooking method says summer more eloquently than barbecuing. Here, meltingly tender barbecued pattypan squash and delicate baby spinach are tumbled in a creamy, citrusy dressing for a colourful summer side dish or light lunch.

12 yellow (baby) pattypan or scallop squash
60 ml (2 fl oz/¼ cup) olive oil
1½ tablespoons crème fraîche
1 tablespoon orange juice
½ teaspoon grated orange zest
1 teaspoon chopped mint, plus 1 small handful leaves
1 small handful baby spinach leaves
1 small handful rocket (arugula)

1. Preheat one burner of a covered barbecue to medium high heat. Put the squash in a foil baking tray and toss with half the olive oil. Season with salt and pepper. Place the tray on a rack over the unlit burner in the barbecue, close the lid and bake by indirect heat for 25-30 minutes, or until tender. Alternatively you can cook the squash in a preheated 200°C (400°F/Gas 6) oven for 25 minutes

2. Meanwhile, put the remaining olive oil, crème fraîche, orange juice, orange zest and chopped mint in a small bowl and mix until smooth. Season with salt and freshly ground black pepper.

3. Cut the squash in half and put in a bowl with the mint leaves, spinach and rocket. Add the dressing and toss to coat. Serve immediately, while the squash are still warm.

Toss the squash in half of the olive oil until well coated.

Mix together the dressing ingredients until smooth.

23 mins

Chargrilled vegetable skewers with harissa and yoghurt

MAKES: 8 SKEWERS ✳ **PREPARATION TIME: 15 MINUTES** ✳ **COOKING TIME: 8 MINUTES**

Harissa
2 teaspoons cumin seeds
½ teaspoon caraway seeds
75 g (2½ oz) large red chillies, chopped
3 garlic cloves, chopped
1 teaspoon sea salt flakes
50 g (1¾ oz) tomato purée (tomato paste)
4 tablespoons olive oil

1 aubergine (eggplant), cut into 2 cm (¾ inch) cubes
150 g (5½ oz) button mushrooms, stems trimmed and sliced in half
250 g (9 oz) cherry tomatoes
1 courgette (zucchini), sliced
125 g (4½ oz/½ cup) Greek-style yoghurt
steamed rice and coriander (cilantro) leaves, to serve

1. Heat a small non-stick frying pan over a medium-high heat and dry-fry the cumin and caraway seeds for 30 seconds, or until fragrant. Place into the bowl of a small food processor with the chillies, garlic, salt, 50 ml (1¾ fl oz) of water and tomato purée. Purée until almost smooth. Gradually add the olive oil and purée until combined.

2. Preheat a barbecue or chargrill plate to medium-high heat. Thread the aubergine, mushrooms, tomatoes and courgette onto metal skewers. Brush generously with half the harissa.

3. Cook the skewers for 5-7 minutes on each side, or until golden. Serve the skewers with the extra harissa, yoghurt, steamed rice and garnished with coriander, if desired.

harissa

Harissa is a North African condiment of chillies and spices— always caraway seeds—used to flavour stews and used to add aromatic heat and red colour to any dish. Store in the refrigerator for up to 6 months. Harissa is available at gourmet food stores and Middle Eastern markets.

Three ways with rocket

Long a staple of Southern Europe, where it grows wild, this powerful little leaf was the culinary rediscovery of the 1990s, leaping easily from restaurant plate to the home kitchen. While it adds a hot little kick to salads, it's also fabulous added to a cooked dish.

Rocket pesto on cheese tortellini

SERVES: 4 ✳ **PREPARATION TIME: 20 MINUTES** ✳ **COOKING TIME: 5 MINUTES**

To make the pesto, put 60 g (2¼ oz/1⅔ cups) baby rocket (arugula), 1 small handful parsley, 2 crushed garlic cloves and 20 g (¾ oz/¼ cup) golden walnuts in a food processor and blend until smooth. Add 35 g (1¼ oz/⅓ cup) finely grated parmesan cheese and mix through. With the motor running, drizzle in 125 ml (4 fl oz/½ cup) olive oil in a thin stream. Season with salt and a little freshly ground black pepper. Stir in enough water (1-1½ tablespoons) to give a good coating consistency. Cook 1kg (2 lb 4 oz) cheese tortellini in a saucepan of boiling salted water according to the manufacturer's instructions. Drain and toss with 2-3 tablespoons of the pesto. Divide among 4 bowls, spoon a little more pesto over each serving and top with shavings of parmesan cheese. Store the remaining pesto in a sealed container in the refrigerator for up to 5 days.

Rocket with butternut squash and gorgonzola dressing

SERVES: 4 ✳ **PREPARATION TIME: 15 MINUTES** ✳ **COOKING TIME: 15 MINUTES**

To make the dressing, mash 50 g (1¾ oz) gorgonzola or other blue cheese with ½ crushed garlic clove in a small food processor. With the motor running, gradually add 1½ tablespoons olive oil, then 3 teaspoons white wine vinegar. Remove from the processor and stir through 60 ml (2 fl oz/¼ cup) cream and ½ teaspoon chopped tarragon. Season with freshly ground black pepper. Peel 500 g (1 lb 2 oz) butternut squash and slice very thinly. Spray a hot chargrill pan with olive oil. Cook butternut squash slices for about 2 minutes on each side, or until cooked. Put 2 large handfuls rocket (arugula) leaves, 2 tablespoons roasted pine nuts, the butterbut squash and the dressing in a bowl and toss together. Serve immediately. Serves 4.

Penne with rocket

SERVES: 4 ✳ **PREPARATION TIME: 15 MINUTES** ✳ **COOKING TIME: 15 MINUTES**

Roughly chop 200 g (7 oz) rocket (arugula) and finely chop 3 tomatoes. Cook 500 g (1 lb 2 oz) penne in a large saucepan of rapidly boiling salted water until al dente. Drain and return to the pan. Place the pan over a low heat. Add 100 g (3½ oz) butter, tossing it through until it melts and coats the pasta. Add the rocket to the pasta along with the tomato. Toss through to wilt the rocket. Stir in 45 g (1¾ oz/½ cup) freshly grated pecorino cheese and season to taste. Serve sprinkled with freshly grated parmesan cheese.

30 mins

Thai red squash curry

SERVES: 4 ∗ PREPARATION TIME: 10 MINUTES ∗ COOKING TIME: 20 MINUTES

Thai cooking uses several kinds of curry pastes, each with a distinct flavour and colour obtained from its blend of herbs and spices. Red curry paste is highly fragrant. The commercial brands vary from medium to hot in intensity, so add more or less to suit your taste.

2 tablespoons oil
1–2 tablespoons Thai red curry
    paste
400 ml (14 fl oz) coconut milk
2 tablespoons soy sauce
125 ml (4 fl oz/½ cup) light
    vegetable stock
2 teaspoons grated palm sugar
700 g (1 lb 9 oz) pattypan (baby)
    squash, halved, or quartered
    if large
100 g (3½ oz) baby corn, halved
    lengthways
100 g (3½ oz) mangetout (snow
    peas), topped and tailed
2 teaspoons lime juice
35 g (1¼ oz/⅓ cup) unsalted
    roasted cashews, coarsely
    chopped
lime wedges to serve (optional)

1. Heat the oil in a large saucepan over medium-high heat and fry the curry paste for 1-2 minutes, or until the paste separates. Add the coconut milk, soy sauce, stock and palm sugar and stir until the sugar has melted. Bring to the boil.

2. Add the squash to the pan and return to the boil. Add the baby corn and simmer, covered, for 12-15 minutes, or until the squash is just tender. Add the mangetout and lime juice and simmer, uncovered, for 1 minute. Serve with cashews scattered over the top, and accompanied by the lime wedges if desired.

Note: If pattypan squash are unavailable, use courgettes (zucchini), cut into slices 2.5cm (1 inch) thick.

pattypan squash

Pattypan (baby) squash belong to the marrow family, which also includes winter squash (pumpkins), cucumbers, melons, and gourds. Fresh and snappy when eaten raw, they are fabulously soft and luscious once cooked. Abundant throughout summer, they may be green and/or yellow in colour. Both the skin and flesh are firmer than those of other summer squash, however, which makes this squash good for baking and stewing.

Aubergine, mozzarella and red pepper stacks

SERVES: 4 ✳ **PREPARATION TIME: 5 MINUTES** ✳ **COOKING TIME: 25 MINUTES**

Mozzarella is a fresh, springy cheese traditionally made with buffalo's milk, although cow's milk is now often used. Mozzarella has an elasticity that makes it excellent for melting, as in this recipe. Buy the mozzarella first, then choose aubergine of roughly the same diameter.

2 small (about 280 g/10 oz each) aubergines (eggplants)
2 small red peppers (capsicums), halved, seeded and roasted
125 ml (4 fl oz/½ cup) olive oil
seasoned plain (all-purpose) flour for dusting
250 g (9 oz) mozzarella (preferably buffalo)
70 g (2½ oz/½ cup) provolone cheese, finely grated
2 teaspoons thyme
1 tablespoon shredded basil

1. Cut each aubergine into six 1.5 cm (⅝ inch) thick rounds.

2. Cut each roasted pepper half into 2 pieces roughly the same shape as the aubergine slices.

3. Heat half the olive oil in a large frying pan until medium-hot. Lightly dust the aubergine slices with the seasoned flour and fry in batches for about 5 minutes, until golden on both sides but still firm, adding more oil as required. Drain on paper towels.

4. Preheat the oven to 200°C (400°F/Gas 6). Cut the mozzarella into twelve 1 cm (½ inch) slices. Grease a small baking dish, about 16 cm (6¼ inches) square and 6 cm (2½ inches) deep. Arrange 4 slices of aubergine in the dish and top each slice with a slice of mozzarella, a sprinkling of provolone and a piece of red pepper. Scatter with some thyme and basil. Repeat this layering once more.

5. Finish with the last of the aubergine, then the mozzarella. Scatter the remaining provolone over the top.

6. Stick a wooden skewer or toothpick through the centre of each stack to keep the layers in place. Bake for 20 minutes, or until the mozzarella has melted and the top is golden brown. Transfer the stacks to 4 serving plates, remove the skewers and serve hot, before the mozzarella cools and becomes rubbery.

Slice each roasted pepper half into two pieces.

Layer the aubergine, mozzarella, provolone and pepper.

Fattoush salad

SERVES: 4 ∗ **PREPARATION TIME: 15 MINUTES** ∗ **COOKING TIME: 5 MINUTES**

A spice used extensively in Lebanese and Turkish cooking, sumac is a dark reddish-purple berry with a distinct tangy citrus flavour. It partners perfectly with roasted vegetables, sprinkled over salads or added to a dressing.

1 large pitta (Lebanese) bread, split
2 baby cos (romaine) lettuces, torn into bite-sized pieces
2 tomatoes, chopped
2 small Lebanese (short) cucumbers, chopped
1 green pepper (capsicum), cut into large dice
4 spring onions (scallions), chopped
1 large handful mint, roughly chopped
1 large handful coriander (cilantro) leaves, roughly chopped

Dressing
3 tablespoons lemon juice
3 tablespoons olive oil
1 tablespoon sumac

1. Preheat the oven to 180°C (350°F/ Gas 4). Place the pitta bread on a baking tray and bake for 5 minutes, or until golden and crisp. Remove from the oven and cool. Break into 2cm (¾ inch) pieces.

2. To make the dressing, mix the lemon juice, oil and sumac together and season to taste.

3. In a serving bowl, toss the lettuce, tomatoes, cucumber, pepper, spring onions and herbs together. Crumble over the toasted pitta bread, drizzle with the dressing and serve immediately.

Herbs should be chopped with a large knife.

Keep the blade end of the knife on the board and rock the handle up and down.

22 mins

Spaghetti with lemon and rocket

SERVES: 4 ＊ **PREPARATION TIME: 15 MINUTES** ＊ **COOKING TIME: 7 MINUTES**

This is one of the simplest and tastiest pasta dishes around, perfect for last–minute summer entertaining. The key is to use the best ingredients available, so that the flavours can truly sing.

375 g (13 oz) spaghetti

100 g (3½ oz) rocket (arugula), finely shredded

1 tablespoon finely chopped lemon zest

1 garlic clove, finely chopped

1 small red chilli, seeded and finely chopped

1 teaspoon chilli oil

5 tablespoons extra virgin olive oil

60 g (2¼ oz) parmesan cheese, finely grated

1. Cook the spaghetti according to the packet instructions until *al dente*. Drain well.

2. Combine the rocket, lemon zest, garlic, chilli, chilli oil, extra virgin olive oil and two-thirds of the grated parmesan in a large bowl and mix together gently.

3. Add the pasta to the rocket and lemon mixture and stir together well. Serve topped with the remaining parmesan and season to taste with salt and cracked black pepper.

> **Note:** If you prefer, you can substitute basil leaves for the rocket.

Three ways with sweetcorn

No vegetable is more emblematic of summer than sweetcorn. The bright yellow kernels and sweet juice conjure memories of the endless summers of childhood, and corn's popularity makes it perfect for summer parties and barbecues.

Corn spoonbread

SERVES: 4 ∗ **PREPARATION TIME: 5 MINUTES** ∗ **COOKING TIME: 25 MINUTES**

Combine 250 g (9 oz/1 cup) crème fraîche, 1 egg, 25g (1oz/¼ cup) grated parmesan cheese and 30 g (1 oz/¼ cup) self-raising flour in a large bowl. Slice the kernels off 3 sweet corn cobs and add to the bowl. Add a pinch of cayenne pepper, and salt and freshly ground black pepper, to taste. Spoon into a greased shallow 18 cm (7 inch) square ovenproof dish. Sprinkle with 2 tablespoons grated parmesan cheese and dot with 40 g (1½ oz) butter. Bake in a preheated 200°C (400°F/Gas 6) oven for 25 minutes, or until set and golden brown. Serve immediately, straight from the dish.

Thai sweetcorn cakes with chilli dipping sauce

MAKES: 12 ∗ **PREPARATION TIME: 20 MINUTES** ∗ **COOKING TIME: 10 MINUTES**

To make the dipping sauce, put 1 tablespoon soy sauce, 2 tablespoons cold water, ½ teaspoon grated palm sugar, 2 teaspoons rice vinegar, 1 seeded and finely chopped red bird's eye chilli and 1 teaspoon finely chopped coriander (cilantro) stems in a small bowl and whisk until the sugar has dissolved. Slice the kernels off 3 medium sweetcorn cobs. You will need 400 g (14 oz/2 cups) in total. Put 200g (7 oz/1 cup) of the corn in a food processor with 2 chopped garlic cloves, 3 teaspoons grated fresh ginger, ½ seeded and chopped large red chilli, 30g (1 oz/¼ cup) plain (all-purpose) flour, ½ teaspoon grated palm sugar, 2 tablespoons coarsely chopped coriander (cilantro) leaves, 1 teaspoon soy sauce and 2 eggs. Process until the mixture is chopped medium-fine. Transfer to a bowl and stir through the remaining corn kernels. Check the seasoning. Heat 60ml (2 fl oz/¼ cup) oil in a large frying pan over medium heat. Spoon heaped tablespoons of the corn mixture into the pan and fry for 1–1½ minutes each side, or until browned. Serve hot with the dipping sauce.

Barbecued sweetcorn, sweet potato and tomatoes with purple basil

SERVES: 4 ∗ **PREPARATION TIME: 15 MINUTES** ∗ **COOKING TIME: 10 MINUTES**

Strip the husks and silks off 2 small sweet corn cobs, halve 4 plum (roma) tomatoes lengthways and peel and thickly slice a 200g (7 oz) sweet potato into rounds. Brush the vegetables with 60 ml (2 fl oz/¼ cup) olive oil. Cook on medium-high heat on a preheated barbecue plate or chargrill pan, 4-5 minutes for the tomatoes and 6-8 minutes for both the corn and the sweet potato. Transfer the tomatoes to a large bowl. Slice the corn into 2 cm (¾ inch) rounds, cut the sweet potato into half moons and add to the tomatoes. Add 1 small handful purple (opal) basil, torn if large. Combine 80 ml (2½ fl oz/⅓ cup) olive oil, 2 tablespoons each of lemon juice and dijon mustard, 1 crushed garlic clove and a pinch of sugar in a small bowl. Season with salt and freshly ground black pepper, to taste. Add 2 tablespoons of the dressing to the vegetables and toss gently. Arrange the corn, tomatoes and sweet potato in a pile on 4 serving plates and drizzle with the remaining dressing.

30 mins

Courgette, thyme and bocconcini pizza

SERVES: 2 * **PREPARATION TIME: 10 MINUTES** * **COOKING TIME: 20 MINUTES**

Courgette is a wondrous vegetable—ubiquitous to the point of being commonplace, but also extremely versatile. Courgette responds just as well to a long slow braise as it does a quick toss in the frying pan. It can also be eaten raw, and is one of the few vegetables that actually goes well in sweet dishes.

2 x ready-made pizza bases

8 courgettes (zucchini), cut into fine rounds

2 teaspoons grated lemon zest

1 large handful finely chopped parsley

2 teaspoons thyme sprigs

4 garlic cloves, crushed

4 tablespoons olive oil

500 g (1lb 2 oz) bocconcini (fresh baby mozarella cheese) cheese, finely diced

50 g (½ cup) grated parmesan cheese

1 tablespoon extra virgin olive oil

1. Preheat the oven to 220°C (425°F/ Gas 7).

2. Place ready-made pizza bases on two pizza trays.

3. Place the courgette rounds, lemon zest, parsley, thyme, garlic and olive oil in a bowl and mix together. Top each pizza base evenly with half the bocconcini and half the parmesan, then spoon on the courgette mixture. Evenly distribute the remaining bocconcini and parmesan over the top, season well with salt and pepper, and drizzle with the extra virgin olive oil. Cook for 15-20 minutes, or until the base is crisp, and the topping is warmed through and golden.

courgettes

Eat courgettes as soon as possible after purchase, as refrigeration makes the texture deteriorate. There is no need to peel them; in fact, most of the flavour is in the skin.

25 mins

Lemongrass and ginger infused fruit salad

SERVES: 4 * PREPARATION TIME: 15 MINUTES * COOKING TIME: 10 MINUTES

Flavoured syrups turn an ordinary fruit salad into something really special. For something a little different try serving this fruit salad on top of a pavlova, in a tropical trifle or inside crepes.

60 g (2¼ oz/¼ cup) caster (superfine) sugar
2 cm x 2 cm (¾ inch x ¾ inch) piece fresh ginger, thinly sliced
1 stalk lemongrass, bruised and halved
1 large passionfruit
1 red pawpaw
½ honeydew melon
1 large mango
1 small fresh pineapple
12 fresh lychees
1 small handful mint leaves, shredded

1. Place the sugar, ginger and lemongrass in a small saucepan, add 125 ml (4 fl oz/½ cup) water and stir over low heat to dissolve the sugar. Boil for 5 minutes, or until reduced to 80 ml (2⅔ fl oz/⅓ cup) and cool. Strain the syrup and add the passionfruit pulp.

2. Peel and seed the pawpaw and melon. Cut into 4 cm cubes. Peel the mango and cut the flesh into cubes discarding the stone. Peel, halve and core the pineapple and cut into cubes. Peel the lychees, then make a slit in the flesh and remove the seed.

3. Place all the fruit in a large serving bowl. Pour on the syrup, or serve separately if preferred. Garnish with the shredded mint.

25 mins

Trifle

SERVES: 6 ✳ **PREPARATION TIME: 15 MINUTES** ✳ **COOKING TIME: 10 MINUTES**

Bursting with colour and flavour, raspberries are not really team players, not where other fruit are concerned at any rate. Instead, they prefer the company of ingredients such as cream, sponge cake, chocolate and champagne. Fresh raspberries are delicate and should be handled as little as possible.

4 slices of madeira (pound) cake or trifle sponges

3 tablespoons sweet sherry or Madeira

250 g (9 oz) raspberries

4 eggs

2 tablespoons caster (superfine) sugar

2 tablespoons plain (all-purpose) flour

500 ml (17 fl oz/2 cups) milk

¼ teaspoon natural vanilla extract

125ml (4 fl oz/½ cup) cream, whipped

3 tablespoons flaked almonds, to decorate

raspberries, to decorate

1. Put the cake in the base of a bowl, then sprinkle it with the sherry. Scatter the raspberries over the top and crush them gently into the sponge with the back of a spoon to release their tart flavour, leaving some of them whole.

2. Mix the eggs, sugar and flour together in a bowl. Heat the milk in a pan, pour it over the egg mixture, stir well and pour back into a clean pan. Cook over medium heat until the custard boils and thickens and coats the back of a spoon. Stir in the vanilla, cover the surface with plastic wrap and leave to cool.

3. Pour the cooled custard over the raspberries and leave to set in the fridge – it will firm up but not become solid. Spoon the whipped cream over the custard. Go wild decorating with almonds and raspberries (or anything else you fancy) and refrigerate until needed.

raspberries

Most raspberries are red, although there are yellow, orange, amber, white and black varieties. Although a more delicate fruit than strawberries, they are interchangeable in most recipes. Raspberries do not ripen when picked, so they should always be bought when fully ripe on the day they are to be eaten.

Caramelised peach and passionfruit crumble tart

SERVES: 6 ✳ **PREPARATION TIME: 10 MINUTES** ✳ **COOKING TIME: 20 MINUTES**

Using ready-made shortcrust (pie) pastry makes this tart a wonderfully quick recipe. Choose a good-quality buttery one and let it sit for 20 minutes before rolling out or it will crack and be difficult to work with. The caramelised peaches bring a mellow richness to this dessert.

20 cm (8 inch) ready-made pastry case

80 g (2¾ oz/⅔ cup) plain (all-purpose) flour

40 g (1½ oz/¼ cup) soft brown sugar

40 g (1½ oz) unsalted butter, chilled and cubed

20 g (¾ oz/¼ cup) desiccated coconut

2 tablespoons chopped roasted skinned hazelnuts

4 peaches, sliced

80 g (2¾ oz/⅓ cup) caster (superfine) sugar

3 passionfruit

1. Preheat the oven to 200°C (400°F/ Gas 6).

2. Rub the flour, brown sugar and butter together. Add the coconut and chopped hazelnuts. Set aside.

3. Heat a frying pan over high heat. Toss the peach slices in the caster sugar. Tip the peaches into the frying pan and cook for 3-4 minutes, moving them occasionally until they are evenly coated in caramel. Add the passionfruit pulp and remove the pan from the heat.

4. Spoon the peach mixture into the pastry case and top with the hazelnut mixture.

5. Bake the tart for 15-20 minutes, or until the crumble top is golden brown.

Add the passionfruit pulp to the caramelised peaches.

Scatter the hazelnut crumble over the top of the tart.

autumn

Autumn is the season of 'mists and mellow fruitfulness', a time of reflection and reconnection after the social whirl of summer. As the days shorten and each evening becomes a little crisper than the last, there comes a yearning for the slow and earthy in all things. Nature has a keener edge as the glitter of summer gives way to the nostalgia of autumnal days. Before our thoughts, and the seasons, turn to the barren months of winter there is one final glorious burst of bounteous fertility as plants make a last-ditch effort to fruit and flower before the cold sets in. This is our chance to slow down in the kitchen and savour the deep, complex flavours of autumn.

The meeting point of summer and winter, autumn straddles the gap between the extremes. Autumn food occupies the same space in our hearts. More substantial than the fast, light dishes of summer, yet still simple; sumptuous and filling, yet not as heavy as the classics of winter — it's about taking the best that nature has to offer and then treating it simply to draw out its essence.

In these mild, darkening months, fields and forests offer an abundance of wild mushrooms; garlic, leeks and onions are at their freshest and sweetest; potatoes, turnips, parsnips and swedes are ready to be pulled from the earth; beetroot, broccoli and borlotti beans are fresh and ready to cook. There is no easier way to judge what is truly in season than to visit your local farmers' market. Even if it's not possible for you to regularly frequent a farmers' market, a visit there will prove an educative and fascinating experience, allowing you to confidently select those vegetables which are truly in season during your weekly supermarket shop.

To bring out the purest flavour of each dish, all you need is a little knowledge and a sure hand. Every cooking technique has its place; it's simply a matter of deciding on the effect you want and treating the vegetable appropriately. Autumn vegetables are versatile, lending themselves to a number of dishes and styles. Beans can be briefly blanched for a warm salad or stewed with tomatoes for a hearty dish; mushrooms can be grilled, fried or baked; and there's almost no end to the culinary uses of the humble yet beloved potato.

So gather the autumn harvest to your heart — this is the season to embrace fecundity and make each meal a generous feast. Let nature set the menu and revel in fresh, seasonal vegetables treated with care and served with love.

30 mins

Butternut squash, spinach and ricotta lasagne

SERVES: 4 ✳ **PREPARATION TIME: 15 MINUTES** ✳ **COOKING TIME: 15 MINUTES**

Choose squashs that are heavy for their size and have unblemished skins. Store whole at room temperature for up to 1 month. Wrap cut squash in plastic wrap and store in the refrigerator.

60 ml (2 fl oz/¼ cup) olive oil

1.5 kg (3 lb 5 oz) butternut squash (pumpkin), cut into 1.5 cm (⅝ inch) dice

500 g (1 lb 2 oz) English spinach leaves, thoroughly washed

4 fresh lasagne sheets (12 x 20 cm/ 5x8 inches)

500 g (1 lb 2 oz/2 cups) ricotta cheese

2 tablespoons cream

25 g (1 oz/¼ cup) grated parmesan cheese

pinch ground nutmeg

1. Heat the oil in a non-stick frying pan over medium heat. Add the squash and toss. Cook, stirring occasionally, for 15 minutes, or until tender (don't worry if the squash is slightly mashed). Season and keep warm.

2. Meanwhile, cook the spinach in a large saucepan of boiling water for 30 seconds, or until wilted. Using a slotted spoon, transfer to a bowl of cold water. Drain well and squeeze out as much excess water as passible. Finely chop the spinach. Add the lasagne sheets to the pan of boiling water and cook, stirring occasionally, until *al dente*. Drain and lay the sheets side-by-side on a clean tea towel. Cut each sheet widthways into thirds.

3. Put the ricotta, cream, parmesan, spinach and nutmeg in a small pan. Stir over low heat for 2-3 minutes, or until warmed through. Work quickly to assemble. Place a piece of lasagne on the base of each plate. Using half the squash, top each of the sheets, then cover with another piece of lasagne. Use half the ricotta mixture to spread over the lasagne sheets, then add another lasagne piece. Top with the remaining squash, then remaining ricotta mixture. Season well and serve immediately.

Chop the spinach very finely with a sharp knife.

30 mins

Mushroom pot pies

SERVES: 4 ✳ PREPARATION TIME: 5 MINUTES ✳ COOKING TIME: 25 MINUTES

Large field mushrooms are packed full of flavour. Look for those with white unblemished skin, and pale gills that haven't darkened or sweated. These days mushrooms come to us in a very clean state. If they are a little dirty, they should be wiped clean with dampened cloth, never washed.

5 tablespoons olive oil
1 leek, sliced
1 garlic clove, crushed
1 kg (2 lb 4 oz) large field
    mushrooms, roughly chopped
1 teaspoon chopped thyme
300 ml (10½ fl oz) cream
1 sheet ready-rolled puff pastry,
    thawed
1 egg yolk, beaten, to glaze

1. Preheat the oven to 220°C (425°F/ Gas 4). Heat oil in a large saucepan over medium heat. Cook the leek, garlic and mushrooms for 5 minutes, or until the leek is soft and translucent and the mushrooms have released their juices and are soft and slightly coloured, then add the thyme.

2. Increase the heat to high and stir in the cream. Cook, stirring occasionally, for 5 minutes, or until the cream has reduced to a thick sauce. Remove from the heat and season well with salt and pepper.

3. Divide the filling among four 315ml (1¼ cup) ramekins or ovenproof bowls. Cut the pastry into rounds slightly larger than the dish. Brush the rim of the ramekins with a little of the egg yolk, place the pastry on top and press down to seal. Brush the top with the remaining egg yolk. Place the ramekins on a metal tray. Bake for 15-20 minutes, or until the pastry has risen and is golden brown.

mushrooms

Store mushrooms in the fridge in a paper bag to allow them to breathe. Don't leave them in plastic as this makes them sweat. Mushrooms do not keep for long. Cultivated mushrooms will last up to 3 days in a fridge and wild mushrooms are best eaten on the day they are picked.

30 mins

Fennel with walnut parsley crust

SERVES: 4 * **PREPARATION TIME: 10 MINUTES** * **COOKING TIME: 20 MINUTES**

The fresh aniseed flavour and crisp texture of raw fennel bulbs make them delicious in salad. Or, for a softer texture and sweeter flavour, the bulbs can be braised or roasted whole; if halved or quartered, they will caramelize beautifully. The gentle flavour of the pretty fronds can subtly spice up fish and vegetable dishes.

2 tablespoons lemon juice
9 small fennel bulbs, halved
  lengthways
1 teaspoon fennel seeds
100 g (3½ oz/1 cup) grated
  parmesan cheese
160 g (2 cups) fresh breadcrumbs
100 g (3½ oz) walnuts
1 tablespoon parsley
2 teaspoons lemon zest
2 garlic cloves, chopped
250 ml (9 fl oz/1 cup) vegetable
  stock
2¼ tablespoons butter

1. Preheat oven to 200°C (400°F/ Gas 6). Bring a large saucepan of water to the boil and add the lemon juice and 1 teaspoon of salt. Cook the fennel in the acidulated water for 5-10 minutes, or until tender, then drain and cool.

2. Meanwhile heat a dry frying pan and roast the fennel seeds over medium heat for 1 minute to release their flavour. Tip the seeds into a food processor, add the Parmesan, breadcrumbs, walnuts, parsley, lemon zest and garlic, and pulse gently to combine. Stir in 2 tablespoons of stock to moisten the mixture.

3. Place the fennel, flat-side up, in an ovenproof ceramic dish and spoon on the stuffing, spreading to completely cover each piece. Pour the remaining stock around the fennel and top each piece with ½ teaspoon of butter. Bake for 15-20 minutes, basting from time to time, or until the top is golden and the fennel is cooked through. Serve drizzled with the braising juices.

fennel

Fennel is best used straight after harvesting. To store fennel, wrap in a damp tea towel (dish towel) and put it in the vegetable crisper of the fridge.

Radicchio with figs and ginger vinaigrette

SERVES: 4 ✳ PREPARATION TIME: 15 MINUTES ✳ COOKING TIME: NIL

With its beautiful deepred colour and mildly bitter taste, treviso radicchio is a wonderfully simple way to spice up a basic salad. This vegetable resembles a red lettuce with elongated leaves.

1 radicchio (red chicory)
1 small curly endive (frisée) lettuce
3 oranges
½ small red onion, thinly sliced into rings
8 small green figs, quartered
3 tablespoons extra virgin olive oil
1 teaspoon red wine vinegar
⅛ teaspoon ground cinnamon
2 tablespoons orange juice
2 tablespoons very finely chopped glace ginger with syrup
2 pomegranates

1. Wash the radicchio and curly endive leaves in cold water, and drain well. Tear any large leaves into pieces.

2. Peel and segment the oranges, discarding all of the pith. Place in a large bowl with the onion rings, salad leaves and figs, reserving 8 fig quarters.

3. Combine the olive oil, vinegar, cinnamon, orange juice and ginger in a small jug. Season to taste with salt and pepper. Pour over the salad and toss lightly.

4. Arrange the reserved figs in pairs over the salad. If you are using the pomegranates, slice them in half and scoop out the seeds with a spoon. Scatter these over the salad before serving.

Variation: A delicious alternative for this salad is to replace the oranges and orange juice with mandarins and mandarin juice when in season.

radicchio

All types of radicchio can be stored in the fridge for several days and keep best wrapped in a damp tea towel (dish towel). As with all leafy vegetables, it is best not to wash radicchio before storing, but to wait until you are ready to use it.

Three ways with beetroot

For those who know beetroot only from tins, trying the fresh variety will open your eyes to a whole new world. The depth of flavour contained in these scarlet globes can only be captured if you start with a suede-skinned raw beetroot.

Beetroot ravioli with sage burnt butter sauce

SERVES: 4 ✻ **PREPARATION TIME: 20 MINUTES** ✻ **COOKING TIME: 10 MINUTES**

Drain 340 g (12 oz) jar baby beetroots in sweet vinegar, then grate it into a bowl. Add 40 g (1½ oz) grated parmesan cheese and 250 g (9 oz) fresh ricotta cheese and mix well. Take 750 g (1 lb 10 oz) fresh lasagne sheets (4 sheets) and lay one sheet of pasta on a flat surface and place evenly spaced tablespoons of the ricotta mixture on the pasta to give 12 mounds – four across and three down. Flatten the mounds of filling slightly. Lightly brush the edges of the pasta sheet and around each pile of filling with water. Place a second sheet of pasta over the top and gently press around each mound to seal and enclose the filling. Using a pasta wheel or sharp knife, cut the pasta into 12 ravioli. Lay them out separately on a lined tray that has been sprinkled with cornmeal. Repeat with the remaining filling and lasagne sheets to make 24 ravioli. Gently remove any air bubbles after cutting so that they are completely sealed. Cook the pasta in a large saucepan of boiling water until *al dente*. Drain, divide among four serving plates and keep warm. Meanwhile melt 200 g (7 oz) chopped butter in a saucepan and cook for 3-4 minutes, or until golden brown. Remove from the heat, stir in 1 small handful torn sage leaves and 2 crushed garlic cloves, and spoon over the ravioli. Sprinkle with shaved parmesan and season with ground pepper.

Beetroot hummus

SERVES: 8 ✻ **PREPARATION TIME: 15 MINUTES** ✻ **COOKING TIME: 4 MINUTES**

Heat 1 tablespoon of olive oil in a frying pan over medium heat and cook 1 chopped large onion for 2-3 minutes, or until soft. Add 1 tablespoon of cumin and cook for a further 1 minute, or until fragrant. Chop 500 g (1 lb 2 oz) cooked beetroot and place in a food processor or blender with the onion mixture, 400 g (14 oz) drained tinned chickpeas, 1 tablespoon tahini, 80 g (⅓ cup) plain yoghurt, 3 crushed garlic cloves, 60 ml (¼ cup) lemon juice and 125 ml (4 fl oz/½ cup) vegetable stock and process until smooth. With the motor running add 60 ml (2 fl oz/¼ cup) olive oil in a thin steady stream. Process until the mixture is thoroughly combined. Serve the hummus with pitta (Lebanese) or Turkish bread.

Fresh beetroot and goat's cheese salad

SERVES: 4 ✻ **PREPARATION TIME: 15 MINUTES** ✻ **COOKING TIME: 5 MINUTES**

Bring a saucepan of water to the boil, add 200 g (7 oz) green beans and cook for 3 minutes, or until just tender. Remove with tongs and plunge into a bowl of cold water. Drain well. Cut 4 cooked beetroot into wedges. To make the dressing, put 1 tablespoon vinegar, 2 tablespoons extra virgin olive oil, 1 crushed garlic clove, 1 tablespoon of capers in brine, rinsed, drained and coarsely chopped, ½ teaspoon salt and ½ teaspoon cracked black pepper in a jar and shake well. Divide the beans and beetroot wedges among four plates. Crumble the goat's cheese over the top and drizzle with the dressing.

30 mins

Cauliflower rarebit

SERVES: 4 ✳ **PREPARATION TIME: 15 MINUTES** ✳ **COOKING TIME: 15 MINUTES**

At its best in autumn, good cauliflower will have compact, tight white heads with no blemishes or discoloration. It will only need brief cooking to give a crisp texture and to bring out the flavour.

8 thick slices ciabatta
1 garlic clove
800 g (1 lb 12 oz) cauliflower, cut into small florets
120 g (1 cup) grated gruyère cheese
120 g (1 cup) grated cheddar cheese
1 tablespoon dijon mustard
2 eggs, beaten
2 tablespoons beer
4 tablespoons cream

1. Turn on the grill (broiler) and toast the ciabatta. Cut the garlic clove in half and rub the cut sides over one side of each slice of ciabatta.

2. Bring a saucepan of water to the boil and cook the cauliflower for about 5 minutes, or until it is tender when you prod it with a knife. Drain it very well.

3. Mix the cheeses, mustard, egg, beer and cream together. Put the toast on a baking tray and arrange some cauliflower on top of each piece. Divide the cheese mixture among the pieces of toast, making sure you coat all the cauliflower.

4. Put the rarebits under the grill and grill them until they are brown and bubbling.

ciabatta

Ciabatta is slipper-shaped Italian bread with a rough, open texture. The loaves are made from a very wet dough, which allows large bubbles to form and also gives a thin crust. Ciabatta is best eaten on the day it is bought or made.

30 mins

Sweet potato and sage risotto

SERVES: 4 ✳ **PREPARATION TIME: 8 MINUTES** ✳ **COOKING TIME: 22 MINUTES**

The skins of sweet potatoes may be orange, purple or cream and the flesh white, apricot or orange, with the texture becoming drier as the colour deepens. For this recipe, use whichever type you prefer, or whatever is available.

50 ml (1¾ fl oz) extra virgin olive oil

1 red onion, cut into thin wedges

600 g (1 lb 5 oz) orange sweet potato, peeled and cut into 2 cm (¾ inch) cubes

440 g (14 fl oz/2 cups) arborio rice

1.25 litres (5 cups) hot vegetable stock

75 g (¾ cup) shredded parmesan cheese

3 tablespoons shredded sage

shaved parmesan cheese, extra, to garnish

1. Heat 3 tablespoons oil in a large saucepan and cook the onion over medium heat for 2-3 minutes, or until softened. Add the sweet potato and rice and stir until well coated in the oil.

2. Add the 125 ml (4 fl oz/½ cup) hot stock, stirring constantly over medium heat until the liquid is absorbed. Continue adding more stock, 125 ml (4 fl oz/½ cup) at a time, stirring constantly for 20 minutes, or until all the stock is absorbed, the sweet potato is cooked and the rice is tender and creamy.

3. Add the parmesan and 2 tablespoons of the sage. Season well and stir to combine. Spoon into four bowls and drizzle with the remaining oil. Sprinkle the remaining sage over the top and garnish with shaved parmesan.

30 mins

Porcini and walnut pasta

SERVES: 4 ∗ **PREPARATION TIME: 15 MINUTES** ∗ **COOKING TIME: 15 MINUTES**

Porcini are considered the kings of mushrooms and have a wonderful intense earthy flavour. The porcini are soaked in water to soften them and then the soaking water is added to the sauce so that none of the flavour is wasted.

20 g (½ oz) or 2 small packets
  porcini
400 g (14 oz) penne
2 tablespoons olive oil
1 onion, finely chopped
2 garlic cloves, crushed
24 button mushrooms, sliced
3 thyme sprigs
90 g (3¼ oz) toasted walnuts,
  roughly chopped
2 tablespoons sour cream
parmesan cheese, grated

1. Put the porcini in a bowl with just enough boiling water to cover them and leave to soak for 10 minutes. If they soak up all the water quickly, add a little more.

2. Cook the penne in a large saucepan of boiling salted water until it is *al dente*, stirring once or twice to make sure the pieces are not stuck together. The cooking time will vary, depending on the brand of pasta. Check the pasta occasionally as it cooks because packet instructions are often too long by a minute or two.

3. Meanwhile, heat the oil in a deep frying pan and fry the onion and garlic together until translucent but not browned. Add the porcini and any soaking liquid, mushrooms and thyme, and keep frying. The mushrooms will give off liquid as they cook so keep cooking until they soak it back up again. Add the walnuts to the frying pan. Toss with the drained penne, stir the sour cream through and season well. Serve with the parmesan.

Toasting walnuts adds colour and brings out sweetness.

Leave the walnuts until they are completely cold before chopping.

30 mins

Butternut squash soup

SERVES: 4 ✳ **PREPARATION TIME: 10 MINUTES** ✳ **COOKING TIME: 20 MINUTES**

Butternut squash is an extremely versatile vegetable that can be paired with many different flavours, making it perfect for soup. For variations try roasting the squash with ground cumin seeds or adding some curry paste, coconut milk and fresh coriander.

500 ml (2 cups) vegetable stock
750 g (1 lb 10 oz) butternut squash
  (pumpkin), cut into 1.5 cm
  (⅝ inch) cubes
2 onions, chopped
2 garlic cloves, halved
¼ teaspoon ground nutmeg
60 ml (2 fl oz/¼ cup) cream

1. Put the stock and 500 ml (2 cups) water in a large heavy-based saucepan and bring to the boil. Add the squash, onion and garlic and return to the boil. Reduce the heat slightly and cook for 15 minutes, or until the squash is soft.

2. Drain the vegetables through a colander, reserving the liquid. Purée the squash mixture in a blender until smooth (you may need to add some of the reserved liquid). Return the squash purée to the pan and stir in enough of the reserved liquid to reach the desired consistency. Season to taste with nutmeg, salt and cracked black pepper.

3. Ladle the soup into four soup bowls and pour some cream into each bowl to create a swirl pattern on the top. Serve with warm crusty bread.

Three ways with sweet potato

Although just a humble tuber, sweet potato retains an aura of the exotic. The various types may have skins of orange, purple or cream, and flesh of white, apricot or orange. Cut the surface of sweet potato into a diamond pattern and roast it with garlic as a perfect side for roast lamb. Add a deep, creamy sweetness to polenta with soft, mashed sweet potato, or grill it with baby leeks and fennel for a seriously yummy side dish.

Diamond-cut roast sweet potato and slivered garlic

SERVES: 4 * **PREPARATION TIME: 10 MINUTES** * **COOKING TIME: 20 MINUTES**

Peel 2 small orange sweet potatoes (about 14 cm/5½ inches long and 6 cm/2½ inches thick) and halve lengthways. Using a strong, sharp knife, make 1cm (½ inch) deep cuts in a diamond pattern in the peeled surface, 1.5-2 cm (⅝-¾ inch) apart. Be careful not to cut all the way through. Place, cut side up, on a baking tray. Combine the juice of half an orange with 1 tablespoon olive oil in a small bowl and season well with salt and freshly ground black pepper. Drizzle all over the sweet potato. Scatter 8-10 rosemary sprigs on top and roast in a preheated 220°C (425°F/Gas 7) oven for 10 minutes. Scatter 2 finely sliced garlic cloves over the sweet potato and bake for a further 10-15 minutes, or until tender. Serves 4.

Creamy sweet potato polenta

SERVES: 4 * **PREPARATION TIME: 10 MINUTES** * **COOKING TIME: 20 MINUTES**

Peel 400 g (14 oz) white sweet potato, cut into 1cm chunks and cook in simmering salted water for about 10 minutes, until tender. Drain and mash with 40 g (1½ oz) butter and 60 ml (2 fl oz/¼ cup) cream. Pour 750 ml (26 fl oz/3 cups) boiling water into a heavy-based saucepan over medium heat. Add 1 teaspoon salt and slowly stir in 110 g (3¾ oz/¾ cup) instant polenta, breaking up any lumps as you stir. Cook over medium-low heat, stirring often, for 5-10 minutes. Stir in sweet potato mash and continue cooking and stirring until the polenta is very thick and pulls away from the side of the pan, about 5 minutes. Remove from the heat and season with salt and white pepper, to taste. Serve with a sprinkling of cayenne pepper on top.

Chargrilled sweet potato with baby leeks and shaved fennel

SERVES: 4 * **PREPARATION TIME: 20 MINUTES** * **COOKING TIME: 10 MINUTES**

Combine 100 ml (3½ fl oz) olive oil, 2 teaspoons chopped mint, 1 crushed garlic clove and plenty of freshly ground black pepper in a bowl. Scrub 1 small narrow (about 400 g/14 oz) orange sweet potato but do not peel. Cut into 1cm (½ inch) slices, then cut the slices into half-moon shapes. Toss in the oil mixture. Trim 400 g (14 oz/2 bunches) baby leeks and cut into 7-8 cm (2¾-3¼ inches) lengths. Add to the sweet potato and toss to coat. Preheat a barbecue or chargrill pan to medium-high and fry the sweet potato for 4-5 minutes. Add the leeks and continue frying for 3-4 minutes, or until the vegetables are tender. Trim 1 baby fennel bulb, reserving a few green fronds. Slice the fennel very thinly or shave it vertically into whole slices and put it in a bowl with the sweet potato and leeks. Thinly slice 1 small red onion and add, along with 80 g (2¾ oz/scant ½ cup) kalamata olives, 60 ml (2 fl oz/¼ cup) olive oil, 1 tablespoon lemon juice, 1 tablespoon mint leaves and the chopped fennel fronds, to the vegetables. Season with salt and black pepper and toss to combine.

Open lasagne of mushrooms, pine nuts and thyme

SERVES: 4 ∗ **PREPARATION TIME: 10 MINUTES** ∗ **COOKING TIME: 15 MINUTES**

Use your favourite type of cap mushrooms, such as chestnut, swiss brown, portobello or even shiitake, as long as they are no bigger than 4cm (1½inches) across. To prepare, cut off the dirty end of the stalks, shake off excess soil and leaves and wipe the caps with a damp cloth.

200 g (7 oz) (2 medium) fresh pasta sheets
80 g (2¾ oz/⅓ cup) butter
1 tablespoon olive oil
300 g (10½ oz/3⅓ cups) assorted mushrooms, sliced
2 garlic cloves, finely sliced
1 tablespoon fresh thyme
1 tablespoon pine nuts, toasted
3 tablespoons double (thick/heavy) cream
3 tablespoons extra virgin olive oil
35 g (1¼ oz/⅓ cup) coarsely shredded pecorino cheese (or use Grana Padano)

1. Put a large saucepan of water on to boil for the pasta and add 1 teaspoon of salt. Cut the lasagne sheets into sixteen 8 cm (3¼ inch) squares. Boil 8 of the squares for 4 minutes, or until *al dente*. Transfer with a slotted spoon to a bowl of cold water. After 15-20 seconds, they should be cool enough to handle. Lay flat on a dry tea towel (dish towel) and cover with another tea towel. It doesn't matter that the squares may have cooked to uneven sizes. Repeat with the remaining pasta squares.

2. Meanwhile heat the butter and olive oil in a large frying pan. Fry the mushrooms over a high heat, stirring often, until golden brown, 3-4 minutes. Add the garlic and thyme and fry for 1 minute. Add the pine nuts, cream and 2 tablespoons of extra virgin olive oil and stir until combined. Remove from the heat and season with freshly ground black pepper. Taste for salt.

3. Preheat the grill (broiler) to medium-high. Place a pasta square in each of 4 shallow pasta bowls. Cover with a heaped tablespoon of mushroom mixture. Repeat twice more then top with the last 4 pasta squares. The pasta doesn't have to be in uniform stacks, nor the piles neat.

4. Drizzle the remaining extra virgin olive oil over the top and scatter with the pecorino. Place the bowls under the heat just long enough for the cheese to start to melt. Serve hot or warm.

Boil the pasta squares, in batches, until *al dente*.

15 mins

Spiced caramelised bananas

SERVES: 4 ∗ **PREPARATION TIME: 10 MINUTES** ∗ **COOKING TIME: 5 MINUTES**

Warm bananas smell wonderful and the spices in this dish make for a deliciously aromatic dessert. For a twist you could cover the bananas in the frying pan with puff pastry and bake in the oven, before turning out for a scrumptious banana tart tatin.

50 g (1¾ oz) unsalted butter
2 tablespoons soft brown sugar
½ teaspoon ground nutmeg
¼ teaspoon ground allspice
4 bananas, peeled and sliced
   lengthways
grated zest and juice of 1 orange
1 tablespoon rum
2 tablespoons lightly roasted
   pecans or walnuts, chopped
freshly grated nutmeg, to sprinkle
ice cream, to serve

1. Put the butter, sugar, nutmeg and allspice in a frying pan over medium heat. Mix until combined and cook for 1 minute, or until the sugar has dissolved. Add the bananas, cut side down, and cook for 2 minutes, or until a little softened.

2. Remove the bananas to a serving plate. Add the orange zest and juice to the frying pan and stir for 2 minutes, or until mixture thickens and is syrupy. Stir in the rum. Spoon the sauce over the bananas. Sprinkle with the chopped nuts and sprinkle with some freshly grated nutmeg. Serve warm with ice cream.

30 mins

Chocolate puddings

SERVES: 4 ∗ **PREPARATION TIME: 15 MINUTES** ∗ **COOKING TIME: 15 MINUTES**

These puddings only take around 15 minutes to cook and should be served immediately so that their luscious gooey centres can be fully appreciated. To ensure a smooth delivery to the table, have everything absolutely ready before you begin.

160 g (5½ oz) dark chocolate, chopped
butter, for greasing
80 g (2¾ oz) caster (superfine) sugar
60 g (2¼ oz) milk chocolate, chopped
4 eggs
cream, to serve

1. Put the oven on to 200°C (400°F/ Gas 6). Put the dark chocolate in a glass bowl and set it above a pan of simmering water. The chocolate will gradually start to soften and look glossy – when it does this, stir it until it is smooth.

2. Grease the inside of four 200ml (7fl oz) ramekins with butter. Add ½ teaspoon of the sugar to each and shake it around until the insides are coated. Divide the chopped milk chocolate among the ramekins.

3. Beat the rest of the sugar with the egg yolks, using electric beaters, for about 3 minutes, or until you have a pale, cream mass. Clean the beaters and dry them thoroughly. Whisk the egg whites until they are thick enough to stand up in peaks.

4. Fold the melted chocolate into the yolk mixture and then fold in the whites. Use a large spoon or rubber spatula to do this and try not to squash out too much air. Divide the mixture among the four ramekins. Bake for 15-20 minutes. The puddings should be puffed and spongelike. Serve immediately with cream.

25 mins

Spiced glazed oranges

SERVES: 4 * **PREPARATION TIME: 10 MINUTES** * **COOKING TIME: 15 MINUTES**

Star anise is native to China and is a star-shaped fruit containing seeds, and has a strong licorice-like flavour. This spice is used extensively in Arabic and Asian cuisine.

250 ml (9 fl oz/1 cup) orange juice, strained
2 tablespoons caster (superfine) sugar
4 star anise
2 cinnamon sticks, broken in half
4 oranges, peeled and cut into 1cm (½ inch slices)
vanilla ice cream, to serve

1. Put the juice, sugar, star anise and cinnamon sticks in a deep-sided frying pan. Stir over low heat for 3 minutes, or until the sugar has dissolved. Bring to the boil, reduce the heat and simmer for 3 minutes, or until the liquid becomes syrupy.

2. Add the orange slices and simmer for a further 7 minutes, or until the oranges have softened slightly and are well coated with the syrup. Serve the oranges warm, drizzled with syrup and a scoop of vanilla ice cream.

oranges

Oranges have come far from their early days, and can be classified along the following lines: blood (vibrant colour, rich and sweet); sweet (good juice, some seeds); navel (easy to peel, full of flavour and nearly always seedless); and bitter Seville (aromatic skin and tart flavour; used in marmalade and liqueurs, and to make orange flower water). When buying, choose oranges that feel heavy and have tight skin. The skin of most commercially available oranges is coated with a wax polish. If you are using the zest, scrub the fruit very well first or, better still, buy organic unpolished oranges.

winter

Winter is a time to cocoon yourself and rediscover the kitchen as the true heart of your home. As the weather grows cold and the evenings draw in, the gently domestic becomes incredibly appealing. Unlike summer, when fresh is king and fast is the order of the day, winter is about seeking comfort in slow, considered food. Pottering in the kitchen becomes a pleasurable way of whiling away a gloomy afternoon, and tackling a complicated recipe is a challenge to relish.

It is so easy to think of winter as a barren time, but one look at the bounty of winter's harvest should dispel that misconception. This is the season in which root vegetables come into their own. Potatoes, parsnips, turnips and carrots are straight from the ground, their skins still dusted with soil. Swiss chard, cabbage and baby brussels sprouts are sweet, crisp and bursting with goodness. Winter squash and jerusalem artichokes are full of flavour, and shallots are the perfect way to add a sweet, piquant edge to the slow-cooked classics of winter fare.

Celebrating the unique rhythm of each season is as much about method as it is about menu. The cosy warmth of a busy oven takes the edge off a chilly day. Bubbling pots of hearty food permeate the house with tempting aromas, whetting appetites and teasing taste buds. Winter is the time when nostalgia and reality come together in the steamy haze of a bustling kitchen.

Slow cooking heightens both the flavour of the food and the anticipation of the diner. Roasting, braising and caramelising bring out the natural sweetness of vegetables, intensifying their flavour. Consider, also, that method applied with forethought can turn a humble vegetable into a masterpiece. Experiment with an unfamiliar ingredient, or try a new way with an old favourite.

Vegetables may not always be the star of the show, but that's no reason for them not to shine. A winter table without an array of perfectly cooked seasonal vegetables is essentially a table bereft, devoid of the life-enhancing vitality of nature's bounty. As winter weather draws you home, take comfort in the face of cold, dark days with honest fare lovingly cooked. Revel in this short respite from the daily diet's health imperatives and indulge in the guilt-free luxury of the winter table.

Parsnip gnocchi

SERVES: 4 ∗ **PREPARATION TIME: 20 MINUTES** ∗ **COOKING TIME: 10 MINUTES**

The distinctive flavour of parsnips is reliant on the icy snap of winter. They convert starch into sugar after sitting in the cold ground for a number of weeks, and the flesh becomes sweeter. Old or large specimens may need to have their tough core removed before cooking.

500 g (1 lb 2 oz) parsnip, cooked and drained
185 g (6½ oz/1½ cups) plain (all-purpose) flour
50 g (1¾ oz/½ cup) fresh grated parmesan cheese

Garlic herb butter
100 g (3½ oz) butter
2 garlic cloves, crushed
3 tablespoons chopped lemon thyme
1 tablespoon finely grated lime zest

1. Mash the cooked parsnip in a bowl until smooth. Sift the flour into the bowl and add half the parmesan. Season and mix to form a soft dough.

2. Divide the dough in half. Using floured hands, roll each half of the dough out on a lightly floured surface into a sausage shape 2cm (¾ inch) wide. Cut each sausage into short pieces, shape each piece into an oval and press the top gently with floured fork prongs.

3. Lower batches of gnocchi into a large saucepan of boiling salted water. Cook for about two minutes, or until the gnocchi rise to the surface. Use a slotted spoon to transfer to serving plates.

4. To make the garlic herb butter, combine all the ingredients in a small saucepan and cook over medium heat for 3 minutes, or until the butter is nutty brown.

5. To serve, drizzle the garlic herb butter over the gnocchi and sprinkle with the remaining parmesan cheese.

The cleanest way to grate lime or lemon zest is to cover the surface of the grater with a piece of greaseproof paper.

Just grate as normal and then pull off the paper.

30 mins

Butter bean casserole

SERVES: 6-8 ∗ **PREPARATION TIME: 5 MINUTES** ∗ **COOKING TIME: 25 MINUTES**

Also called lima beans, these large flat kidney shaped beans are mild in flavour and popular in Greek and Spanish cooking. They make a great addition to a casserole and also make fabulous creamy dips.

1 large onion, sliced
1 small carrot, chopped
1 small celery stalk, chopped
60 ml (2 fl oz/¼ cup) olive oil
1 garlic clove, chopped
400 g (14 oz) tinned good-quality crushed tomatoes
1 tablespoon tomato purée (tomato paste)
2 x 440g (15½ oz) tins butter beans (lima beans), drained and rinsed
2 teaspoons chopped dill
extra virgin olive oil, for serving

1. Preheat the oven for 180°C (350°F/ Gas 4).

2. Heat the oil in a 2.5 litre (88 fl oz/ 10 cup) flameproof casserole dish over medium heat. Add the onion, garlic, carrot and celery, and cook for 3-4 minutes, or until the onion is translucent. Add the tomatoes, tomato paste and 125 ml (4 fl oz/½ cup) water. Bring to the boil, then reduce the heat and simmer for 2-3 minutes.

3. Add the butterbeans and dill to the casserole dish, then season to taste. Bring back to the boil, then cover and bake for 20 minutes, or until the sauce is thick. Serve hot or at room temperature, drizzled with the oil.

30 mins

Carrot and ginger soup

SERVES: 4 ✳ **PREPARATION TIME: 10 MINUTES** ✳ **COOKING TIME: 20 MINUTES**

In the darkest depths of winter this soup is a great tonic for boosting the immune system, with carrots being high in vitamin A and ginger providing good antioxidant qualities.

750 ml (3 cups) vegetable stock
1 tablespoon oil
1 onion, chopped
1 tablespoon grated fresh ginger
1 kg (2 lb 4 oz) carrots, chopped
2 tablespoons chopped coriander (cilantro) leaves

1. Place the stock in a pan and bring to the boil. Heat the oil in a large heavy-based pan, add the onion and ginger and cook for 2 minutes, or until the onion has softened.

2. Add the stock and carrots. Bring to the boil, then reduce the heat and simmer for 10-15 minutes, or until the carrot is cooked and tender.

3. Place in a blender or food processor and process in batches until smooth. Return to the pan and add a little more stock or water to thin the soup to your preferred consistency.

4. Stir in the coriander and season to taste. Heat gently before serving.

carrots

Most carrots are orange but some are yellow or even purple in colour. Carrots are used to give flavour to soups and stews and are eaten raw as crudités and in salads. They are also used in fresh pickles.

23 mins

Pear and walnut salad with blue cheese dressing

SERVES: 4 * PREPARATION TIME: 20 MINUTES * COOKING TIME: 3 MINUTES

This classic flavour combination is a marriage made in heaven. Corella pears are small with a pretty green skin and pink blush; their firm, white flesh has a rich lushness to it that is complemented by the sharp, tangy flavour of the blue cheese and the crunch of the walnuts.

Dressing
100 g (3 ½ oz) creamy blue cheese
60 ml (2 fl oz/¼ cup) olive oil
1 tablespoon walnut oil
1 tablespoon lemon juice
1 tablespoon cream
2 teaspoons finely chopped sage

100 g (3½ oz/1 cup) walnut halves
4 firm, ripe small pears, such as corella
2 tablespoons lemon juice
2 chicory (witlof or endive), trimmed and leaves separated
100 g (3½ oz/1 cup) parmesan cheese, shaved

1. To make the dressing, purée the blue cheese in a small processor, then add the olive oil, walnut oil and lemon juice, and blend until smooth. With the motor running, slowly add 2 teaspoons warm water. Stir in the cream and sage, and season to taste.

2. Preheat the grill to medium-hot. Place the walnuts in a bowl and cover with boiling water. Allow to steep for 1 minute, then drain. Spread the walnuts on a baking tray and place under the grill for 3 minutes, or until lightly toasted, Chop coarsely.

3. Thinly slice across the pears through the core to make rounds. Do not peel or core the pears, but discard the seeds. As each pear is sliced, sprinkle with a little lemon juice to prevent discoloration. On each serving plate, arrange three pear slices in a circle. Top with a scattering of walnuts, a couple of endive leaves, a few more walnuts and some parmesan. Repeat this layering, reserving the last layer of parmesan and some of the walnuts. Spoon some dressing over each stack, scatter with the remaining walnuts, and top each with the reserved parmesan. Serve as a first course, or as an accompaniment to simple meat dishes.

pears

Though pears are available for much of the year, they are at their best, and in greatest variety, over autumn. Popular choices include the soft and juicy beurre bosc pear; the slow-ripening, juicy packham pear; and the aromatic william (bartlett) pear, which is ideal for cooking. When buying, choose smooth, firm but not hard pears.

Three ways with broccoli

Childhood exhortations to 'eat up your broccoli' have landed this vegetable with an undeserved reputation. Not just extremely good for you, broccoli is also delicious and, when prepared properly, should tempt even the most reluctant eater. Shallots and chestnuts bring a nutty edge to simply steamed broccoli. Mix finely chopped broccoli with creamy ricotta for a light and fluffy dish of yummy goodness, or up the breakfast ante with scrambled eggs and broccoli.

Broccoli, shallots and chestnuts

SERVES: 4 * **PREPARATION TIME: 10 MINUTES** * **COOKING TIME: 20 MINUTES**

Boil 200 g (7 oz/3⅓ cups) small broccoli florets in a large pan of boiling salted water for 3-4 minutes. Remove with a slotted spoon. Add 100 g (3½ oz) frozen peeled chestnuts to the boiling water and cook for 10-12 minutes, or until tender (the chestnuts may break up). Drain the chestnuts. Heat 60 ml (2fl oz/¼ cup) oil in a large frying pan over high heat. Fry 2 thin slices pancetta for about 1 minute, until crisp. Drain on paper towels. Wipe out the pan and heat 2 teaspoons olive oil over low heat. Add 3 quartered, peeled French shallots and 1 crushed garlic clove. Fry for 4-5 minutes, or until softened. Stir in the chestnuts and cook for 2 minutes. Add the broccoli and 1 teaspoon hazelnut oil and cook until heated through. Break the pancetta into strips and add to the pan along with some freshly ground black pepper.

Almond and broccoli stir-fry

SERVES: 4 * **PREPARATION TIME: 10 MINUTES** * **COOKING TIME: 5 MINUTES**

Lightly crush 1 teaspoon coriander seeds using a mortar and pestle or with a rolling pin. Cut 500g (1 lb 2 oz) broccoli into small florets. Heat 60 ml (2 fl oz/¼ cup olive oil) in a wok or a large heavy-based frying pan and swirl to coat the base and side. Add the coriander seeds and 2 tablespoons of slivered almonds. Stir quickly over medium heat for 1 minute, or until the almonds are golden. Add 1 crushed clove of garlic, 1 teaspoon finely shredded fresh ginger and broccoli to the pan. Stir-fry over high heat for 2 minutes. Remove the pan from the heat. Combine 2 tablespoons red wine vinegar, 1 tablespoon soy sauce and 2 teaspoons sesame oil together, pour into the pan. Toss until the broccoli is well coated. Serve immediately, sprinkled with 1 teaspoon toasted sesame seeds.

Broccoli with scrambled eggs

SERVES: 4 * **PREPARATION TIME: 10 MINUTES** * **COOKING TIME: 15 MINUTES**

Cook 400 g (14 oz/6⅔ cups) broccoli florets with some tender stems attached in boiling salted water for 5-8 minutes, or until just tender, then drain. Heat 60 ml (2 fl oz/¼ cup) light olive oil in a frying pan over medium heat. Fry 1 peeled garlic clove and 1 chopped, seeded red bird's eye chilli for 2 minutes. Add the broccoli and toss to coat. Heat for 1 minute, shaking the pan to prevent sticking. Discard the garlic. Push the broccoli to one side of the pan. Combine 2 eggs and 2 tablespoons grated pecorino cheese and season lightly with salt and freshly ground black pepper. Add to the pan and stir with a fork until creamy, but not yet set. Incorporate the broccoli and toss lightly. Serve immediately.

30 mins

Carrot and parsnip roulade

SERVES: 8-10 ✳ **PREPARATION TIME: 15 MINUTES** ✳ **COOKING TIME: 15 MINUTES**

Many people associate roulades with sweet dishes, but they also make incredibly tasty savoury dishes, guaranteed to impress dinner guests.

2 small carrots, roughly chopped and cooked
1 parsnip, roughly chopped and cooked
20 g (¾ oz) butter
10 sage leaves, roughly chopped
1 tablespoon chopped flat-leaf (Italian) parsley
4 eggs, separated
50 g (1¾ oz/½ cup) finely grated parmesan cheese
250 g (9 oz/1 cup) ricotta cheese
2 tablespoons snipped chives

1. Lightly grease a 33 x 25 cm (13 x 10 inch) Swiss roll tin (jelly roll tin) and line the base and sides with baking paper. Preheat the oven to 190°C (375°F/ Gas 5).

2. In a food processor combine cooked carrots and parsnips, butter, sage and parsley and process until smooth. Season, add the egg yolks and process to combine. Tip the mixture into a large bowl.

3. In a separate clean bowl beat the egg whites until soft peaks form. Using a large metal spoon fold a quarter of the egg white into the carrot mixture, then add the rest, stirring gently until just combined. Spoon into the prepared tin and smooth the surface. Bake for 15 minutes, or until it starts to turn golden.

4. Turn the roulade onto a greased sheet of baking paper placed over a tea towel (dish towel), then remove the sheet of baking paper used to line the tin. Sprinkle with half the parmesan and allow to cool slightly.

5. Mix together the ricotta, chives and remaining parmesan and season to taste. Spread the mixture evenly over the roulade and roll it lengthways like a Swiss roll (jelly roll), using the baking paper to gently roll it. Serve immediately with steamed greens or a tossed salad.

Potato tortilla

SERVES: 6-8 * **PREPARATION TIME: 5 MINUTES** * **COOKING TIME: 25 MINUTES**

This classic dish from Spain is winter comfort food at its best, with the simple combination of potato, onion, garlic and eggs. For something different try adding some mushrooms, peas or cherry tomatoes.

**500 g (1 lb 2 oz) potatoes, cut into
    1 cm (½ inch) slices
60 ml (2 fl oz/¼ cup) olive oil
1 brown onion, thinly sliced
4 garlic cloves, thinly sliced
2 tablespoons finely chopped
    flat-leaf (Italian) parsley
6 eggs**

1. Place the potato slices in a large saucepan, cover with cold water and bring to the boil over high heat. Boil for 5 minutes, then drain and set aside.

2. Meanwhile heat the oil in a deep-sided non-stick frying pan over medium heat. Add the onion and garlic and cook for 5 minutes, or until the onion softens. Add the potato to the pan, mixing gently to combine.

3. Whisk the eggs with 1 teaspoon each of salt and freshly ground pepper and pour evenly over the potato mixture. Cover and cook over low-medium heat for 15-20 minutes, or until the egg is just set. Slide onto a serving plate or serve directly from the pan.

Use a mandolin for even slices.

If cutting by hand, use a good, long, sharp knife.

30 mins

Jerusalem artichoke and roast garlic soup

SERVES: 4 * **PREPARATION TIME: 10 MINUTES** * **COOKING TIME: 20 MINUTES**

To stop them going brown, Jerusalem artichokes should be put in acidulated water once cut, and always cooked in a non-reactive pan.

1 garlic head, roasted and skins removed
2 tablespoons butter
1 tablespoon olive oil
1 onion, chopped
1 leek, white part only, washed and chopped
1 celery stalk, chopped
700 g (1 lb 9 oz) Jerusalem artichokes, peeled and chopped into 1 cm (½ inch) cubes
1 small potato, chopped into 1 cm (½ inch) cubes
1.5 litres (52 fl oz/6 cups) hot vegetable stock
olive oil, to serve
finely snipped chives, to serve

1. In a large heavy-based saucepan, heat the butter and oil. Add the onion, leek and celery and a large pinch of salt, and cook for 5 minutes, or until soft. Add the Jerusalem artichokes, potato and garlic and cook for a further 5-10 minutes. Pour in the stock, bring the mixture to the boil, then reduce the heat and simmer for 10-15 minutes, or until the vegetables are soft.

2. Purée in a blender until smooth, and season well. Serve with a drizzle of olive oil and some chives. Delicious with warm crusty bread.

Three ways with cabbage

Forget the cabbage soup diet, put away images of institutional cooking and rediscover the true beauty of the humble cabbage. Make something different for the buffet with this spicy Asian coleslaw. Experts at making something out of nothing, the Irish invented one of the most delicious of winter indulgences, colcannon. It's just cabbage and mash with plenty of butter, but the whole is so much more than the sum of its parts.

Asian-style coleslaw

SERVES: 4 * **PREPARATION TIME: 20 MINUTES** * **COOKING TIME: NIL**

Combine 200 g (7 oz/2⅔ cups) finely shredded red cabbage and 175 g (6 oz/2⅓ cups) finely shredded Chinese cabbage in a large bowl. Peel 1 large carrot and shave it with a vegetable peeler. Thinly slice 1 small red onion and 1 seeded medium red chilli (optional) lengthways. Add the carrot, onion and chilli to the bowl, along with 80 g (2¾ oz/¾ cup) thinly sliced mangetout (snow peas), 1 small handful torn Thai (holy) basil and 2 tablespoons coarsely chopped roasted peanuts and toss to combine. To make the dressing, put 2 tablespoons lime juice, 1½ teaspoons finely grated fresh ginger, 90 g (3¼ oz/⅓ cup) light sour cream, 1 teaspoon soy sauce and 1 crushed garlic clove in a small bowl and whisk until combined. Pour over the cabbage mixture and toss well to coat. Scatter 2 tablespoons coarsely chopped roasted peanuts on top. Serve at room temperature.

Colcannon

SERVES: 4 * **PREPARATION TIME: 10 MINUTES** * **COOKING TIME: 20 MINUTES**

Peel and chop 500 g (1 lb 2 oz) boiling potatoes into 1 cm (½ inch) cubes. Boil in a saucepan of salted water for 10 minutes, or until tender, then drain. Add 40 g (1½ oz) butter and 60 ml (2 fl oz/¼cup) milk, and salt and freshly ground black pepper, to taste. Mash until smooth. Meanwhile heat 40 g (1½ oz) butter in a frying pan over low heat and fry the white part of 1 sliced leek for 4-5 minutes, or until soft but not brown. Add 400 g (14 oz/5⅓ cups) shredded curly kale or savoy cabbage and cook, stirring, for 5-7 minutes, or until softened. Add the potato and a pinch of ground nutmeg and toss to combine. Check the seasoning before serving.

Butter baked baby cabbage

SERVES: 4 * **PREPARATION TIME: 10 MINUTES** * **COOKING TIME: 20 MINUTES**

Cut 1 baby cabbage (about 500 g/1 lb 2 oz) into 4 wedges and place, cut side up, in a small baking dish. Add 2 tablespoons vegetable stock or water. Melt 50 g (1¾ oz) butter in a small saucepan and stir in a large pinch each of ground ginger and sweet paprika. Drizzle over the cabbage wedges and place a thyme sprig on each. Bake in a preheated 200°C (400°F/Gas 6) oven for 20 minutes, or until tender and a little crispy around the edges. If not quite cooked, cover with foil and bake for a further 10-15 minutes. Spoon any pan juices over the top for serving.

30 mins

Orecchiette with broccoli

SERVES: 6 ✳ **PREPARATION TIME: 10 MINUTES** ✳ **COOKING TIME: 20 MINUTES**

In Italian orechiette means 'little ears' and is a traditional pasta of Puglia, commonly served with broccoli.

750 g (1 lb 10 oz) broccoli, cut into florets
450 g (1 lb) orecchiette
60 ml (2 fl oz/¼ cup) extra virgin olive oil
½ teaspoon dried chilli flakes
30 g (1 oz/⅓ cup) grated pecorino or parmesan cheese

1. Blanch the broccoli in a saucepan of boiling salted water for 5 minutes, or until just tender. Remove with a slotted spoon, drain well and return the water to the boil. Cook the pasta in the boiling water until *al dente*, then drain well and return to the pan.

2. Meanwhile, heat the oil in a heavy-based frying pan and add the chilli flakes and broccoli. Increase the heat to medium and cook, stirring, for 5 minutes, or until the broccoli is well coated and beginning to break apart. Season. Add to the pasta, toss in the cheese and serve.

Rhubarb and berry crumble

SERVES: 4 * **PREPARATION TIME: 8 MINUTES** * **COOKING TIME: 22 MINUTES**

Most children blanch at rhubarb. perhaps because it looks like a vegetable — and is in fact botanically classified as such. But with maturity comes a new-found appreciation of the tender pink stalks — particularly when paired with berries, orange and crumble.

850 g (1 lb 4 oz) rhubarb, cut into 2.5 cm (1 inch) lengths
150 g (5½ oz/1¼ cups) frozen blackberries
1 teaspoon grated orange zest
250 g (1 cup) caster (superfine) sugar
125 g (9 oz/1 cup) plain (all purpose) flour
115 g (4 oz/1 cup) ground almonds
½ teaspoon ground ginger
150 g (5½ oz) chilled unsalted butter, cubed

1. Preheat the oven to 200°C (400°F/ Gas 6), and grease a deep 1.5 litre ovenproof dish. Bring a saucepan of water to the boil over high heat, add the rhubarb, and cook for 2 minutes, or until just tender. Drain well and combine with the berries, orange zest and 90 g (3 ¼ oz/⅓ cup) of the caster sugar if needed. Spoon the fruit mixture into the prepared dish.

2. To make the topping, combine the flour, ground almonds, ginger and the remaining sugar. Rub the butter into the flour mixture with your fingertips until it resembles coarse breadcrumbs. Sprinkle the crumble mix over the fruit, pressing lightly. Don't press it down too firmly, or it will become flat and dense.

3. Put the dish on a baking tray and bake for 20-25 minutes, or until the topping is golden and the fruit is bubbling underneath. Leave for 5 minutes, then serve with cream or ice cream.

Note: Substitute raspberries, loganberries or blueberries for the blackberries. Strawberries do not work well as they become too soft when cooked.

Cut the trimmed rhubarb stalks into short lengths.

Individual sticky date cakes

SERVES: 6 ∗ **PREPARATION TIME: 10 MINUTES** ∗ **COOKING TIME: 20 MINUTES**

For food on the move, the date is difficult to beat — an instant boost of energy with its high sugar content, and a little protein, vitamins and minerals thrown in.

270 g (9½ oz/1½ cups) pitted dates, chopped
1 teaspoon bicarbonate of soda
150 g (5½ oz) unsalted butter, chopped
185 g (6½ oz/1½ cups) self-raising flour
265 g (9½ oz) brown sugar
2 eggs, lightly beaten
2 tablespoons golden syrup (dark corn syrup)
185 ml (6 fl oz/¾ cup) cream

1. Preheat the oven to 180°C (350°F/ Gas 4). Grease six 250 ml (9 fl oz/1 cup) muffin tin holes. Place the dates and bicarbonate of soda in a small bowl, pour over 250 ml (9 fl oz/1 cup) boiling water in a saucepan, leave to stand for 10 minutes. Add 60 g (2 ¼ oz/¼ cup) of the butter and stir until melted.

2. Sift the flour into a large bowl, then stir in 125 g (4½ oz/½ cup) of the sugar. Make a well in the centre, add the date mixture and egg and stir until combined. Evenly divide the mixture among the muffin holes and bake for 20 minutes, or until a skewer comes out clean when inserted into the centre.

3. Meanwhile to make the sauce, put the golden syrup, cream, the remaining butter and sugar in a small saucepan and stir over low heat for about 4 minutes, or until the sugar has dissolved. Bring to the boil, then reduce the heat and simmer, stirring occasionally, for 2 minutes.

4. To serve, put the warm cakes onto serving plates, pierce a few times with a skewer and drizzle over the sauce. Serve with ice cream, if desired.

dates

Select dates which haven't been pre-packaged (typically on small trays, wrapped tightly in plastic wrap) as it is difficult to tell their condition. Choose dates that are plump, with unbroken, slightly wrinkled skins. Avoid any with sugary surfaces as this indicates their sugars are crystallizing (due to inappropriate storing or age). Store dates in a sealed container in the refrigerator. Fresh dates will keep for 12 months— they can also be frozen for several years.

30 mins

Orchard fruit compote

SERVES: 4 * **PREPARATION TIME: 15 MINUTES** * **COOKING TIME: 15 MINUTES**

To add colour and contrats to a winter fruit salad, dried fruits make a fantastic addition and absorb the flavours of cooking and soaking liquids brilliantly. The smokey flavour of the lapsang souchong tea adds depth of texture that is complimented perfectly by the spices and the sweetness of the dessert wine.

6 pitted prunes

3 dried peaches, halved

5 dates, seeded and halved

10 dried apricots

1 lapsang souchong tea bag

90 g (¼ cup) honey

½ teaspoon ground ginger

1 cinnamon stick

3 whole cloves

pinch ground nutmeg

750 ml (26 fl oz/3 cups) dessert wine such as sauternes

1 lemon

2 golden delicious apples, peeled and cored

2 beurre bosc pears, peeled and cored

400 g (14 fl oz) Greek-style plain yoghurt

1. Place the prunes, peaches, dates, apricots and tea bag in a large heatproof bowl. Cover with boiling water, and leave to soak. Drain the dried fruit and remove the tea bag.

2. Meanwhile, place the honey, ginger, cinnamon stick, cloves, nutmeg and wine in a saucepan. Peel a large piece of zest from the lemon and place in the pan. Squeeze the juice from the lemon to give 60 ml (2 fl oz/¼ cup) and add to the pan. Cut the apples and pears into pieces about the same size as the dried fruits. Add to the syrup, along with the drained dried fruits. Bring to the boil, stirring, then simmer for 8-10 minutes, or until tender.

3. Remove all the fruit from the pan with a slotted spoon and place in a serving dish. Return the pan to the heat, bring to the boil, then reduce the heat and simmer for 5 minutes, or until the syrup has reduced by half. Pour over the fruit compote and serve hot or cold. Serve with the yoghurt.

index

A READER'S DIGEST BOOK

Published by The Reader's Digest Association Limited
11 Westferry Circus
Canary Wharf
London E14 4HE
www.readersdigest.co.uk

We are committed both to the quality of our products and the service we provide to our customers. We value your comments, so please do call us on 08705 113366, or via our website at www.readersdigest.co.uk. If you have any comments about the content of any of our books, you can contact us at gbeditorial@readersdigest.co.uk

This book was designed, edited and produced by Murdoch Books Pty Limited.

Series Food Editor: Fiona Roberts
Designer: Joanna Byrne
Design Concept: Uber Creative
Production: Monique Layt

Printed by Midas Printing (Asia) Ltd. PRINTED IN CHINA.

IMPORTANT: Those who might be at risk from the effects of salmonella poisoning (the elderly, pregnant women, young children and those suffering from immune deficiency diseases) should consult their doctor with any concerns about eating raw eggs.

CONVERSION GUIDE: You may find cooking times vary depending on the oven you are using. For fan-assisted ovens, as a general rule, set the oven temperature to 20°C (35°F) lower than indicated in the recipe. We have used 20ml (4 teaspoon) tablespoon measures. If you are using a 15ml (3 teaspoon) tablespoon for most recipes the difference will not be noticeable.

Book code: 410-715 UP0000-1
ISBN: 978 0 276 44 266 7
Oracle code: 250011999H